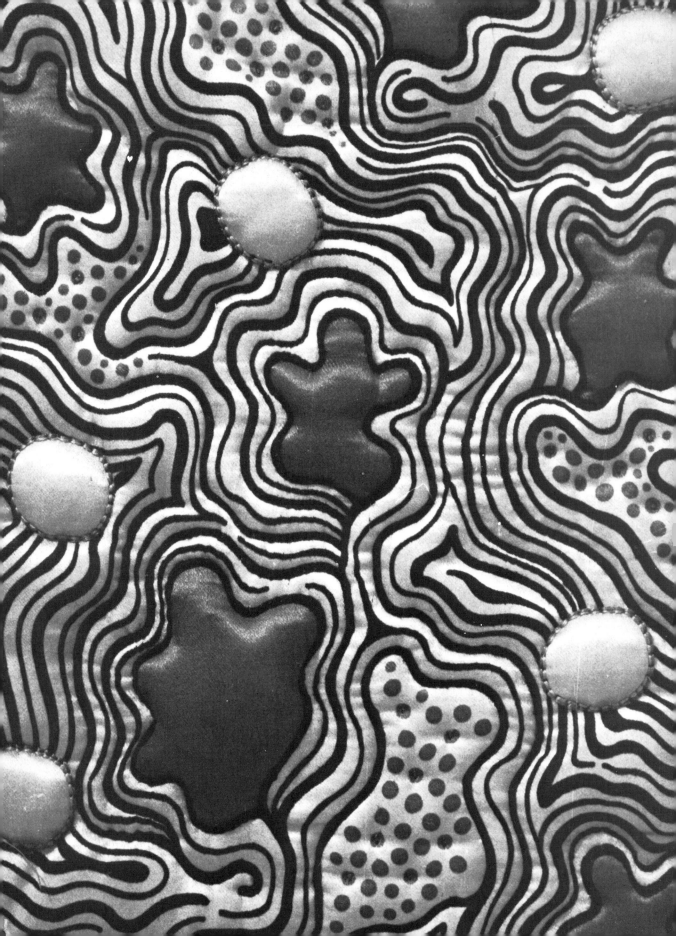

QUILTING
technique, design and application

QUILTING

technique, design and application

Eirian Short

B T Batsford Limited   London

Copyright © Eirian Short 1974
First published 1974
Reprinted 1979, 1981, 1983
First published in paperback 1989

ISBN 0 7134 1541 X

Printed in Great Britain by
The Anchor Press Ltd, Tiptree, Essex
for the publishers
B T Batsford Limited
4 Fitzhardinge Street, London W1H 0AH

Contents

Acknowledgment

I should like to thank The Embroiderers' Guild for permission to reproduce figure 92; the Victoria and Albert Museum for figures 9 and 54; the North Carolina Museum of Art for figure 169 and Averil Colby and Mrs Nigel Morgan for figure 37.

As usual, principals of colleges and heads of departments have been most helpful in allowing students' work to be used, supplying photographs, or lending work for me to photograph. For this I am most grateful. Thanks go to G Cunliffe at the College of All Saints for permission to use fig 58; to Derrick Turner and June Tiley at Cardiff College of Art for fig 129; to Michael Pattrick and Colleen Farr at the Central School of Art and Design for figure 156; to Jon Thompson and Audrey Walker at Goldsmiths' College for figures 10, 30, 32, 35, 57, 67, 80, 81, 82, 83, 84, 85, 87, 89, 108, 109, 110, 111, 128, 161, 162; to A Saunders and Roger Limbrick at the London College of Furniture for figure 158; to RER Downing and Anne Butler at the Embroidery School, Manchester Polytechnic for figures 8, 31, 39, 40, 41, 42, 55, 163.

I am also most grateful to Jacqueline Ayling, Evie Edwards, Eve Lindsey, Anne Preston, Julia Roberts, Barbara Siedlecka and Maureen Whyberd for examples of their work. Special thanks go to the following American artists who sent me photographs of their work: Doris Hoover, Jody Klein, Bets Ramsey, Joan Schulze and Joy Stocksdale.

I should like to thank my husband, Denys Short, who took a great many of the photographs and who was always willing to leave his own work to help me. Lastly, my grateful thanks to Rozanne Hawksley, who collaborated with me on the section of the book which deals with clothes and accessories. Her technical knowledge of pattern cutting and her beautiful pages of drawings are a major contribution to the book.

Camberwell 1979   ES

Suggestions for the use of quilting
on clothes   Maureen Whyberd

12

Introduction

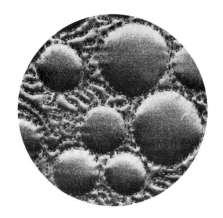

Quilting consists of two or more layers of fabric stitched through by hand or machine, to form a decorative surface pattern. It falls into several distinct categories, often referred to by geographical labels such as 'English' and 'Italian' which are quite unjustified, as quilting is common to nearly all countries and was practised long before England or Italy existed as such. I have therefore adopted the method advocated by Averil Colby in her book *Quilting* and classified each type of quilting by the technique used rather than by the supposed place of origin. Under this system the four main categories are as follows:

1   Wadded quilting

wadded quilting
also known as English and American quilting

This is the oldest form of quilting, based on the securing together of several layers of material to provide protection against cold and discomfort. Wadded quilting consists of a top fabric and backing between which is sandwiched a filling of whatever thickness is required, depending on what the end product is to be. These are some suggestions for its application:

On dress   For extra warmth in housecoats, waistcoats, coat linings, dressing jackets, windcheaters, slippers; for added weight round hems of skirts and evening coats; as decorative detailing on otherwise plain garments, in the form of cuffs, collars, revers or pockets; as accessories in the form of hats, caps, belts, bags, etc.
In the home   For extra warmth as bedcovers, draughtproof curtains, teapot or coffeepot covers; for added comfort on hard benches, un-upholstered chairs and on bedheads; as interesting textural decoration on cushions, pillows, mirror frames, jewel boxes, work boxes, etc.

Further suggestions for use of quilting
on clothes   Maureen Whyberd

3 *Homage to the Square and Joseph
Albers*. Wall Hanging, cotton,
(114 cm × 114 cm: 45 in. × 45 in.)
Bets Ramsey

4 Flat quilting

flat quilting

This has no padding but is merely stitching taken through two layers of fabric. Apart from its value as decoration, its main function is, in dress, to give added weight to a flimsy fabric, and harder wearing qualities at points of friction such as cuffs, collars and pockets; and, in the home, on large articles such as bedcovers and curtains, to strengthen and enliven big, plain areas of 'background' between scattered embroidered motifs.

5 Corded quilting

corded quilting

also known as Italian quilting

Used in an open linear design, corded quilting fulfils much the same function as flat quilting, but if whole areas are corded solidly the resulting quality is more like that of wadded quilting. In this form it can be used in conjunction with stuffed quilting or embroidered motifs to form the entire background to a bed quilt, combining warmth and weight with a rich texture. All corded quilting designs are based on parallel pairs of lines which are stitched through two fabrics to form channels, through which the cord is threaded to make a raised pattern.

stuffed quilting

also known as Trapunto

Stuffed quilting, like corded quilting, is padded after the stitching is complete, making it particularly suitable for carrying out large projects on the machine, when wadded quilting becomes unmanageable. It consists of enclosed shapes padded from behind to stand out in high relief on the right side of the work. Its main application is as a decoration, but, like corded quilting, if massed together it will take on some of the qualities of wadded quilting. Different types of quilting may be put together in various combinations. For instance, on a design in wadded quilting, certain focal points could be emphasised by additional stuffing. Alternatively, stuffed and corded quilting may be combined to give a balanced mixture of solid and linear elements in a design.

6   Stuffed quilting

Any of the above techniques when worked on transparent fabrics are known as 'Shadow Quilting' and, when coloured fillings which show through the top fabric are used, an added interest is given to the work.

Quilting can be combined with other forms of embroidery such as surface stitchery, beading, appliqué etc. Whether these are worked before or after the quilting process will depend on individual cases, though generally speaking, appliqué would be worked before quilting, beading afterwards, etc. Also included in the book are some techniques which, without being true quilting, are closely enough related to it to merit inclusion. Some, for instance tied and gathered quilting, are offshoots of traditional methods; others, such as pillow quilting, are modern, time-saving short cuts. One method does away with stitching altogether, making use of an iron-on interlining to bond the layers together. This is, of course, more limited in its application as it would not stand up to the laundering or dry cleaning necessary for garments or soft furnishings. It has a part to play, however, in the use of quilted effects in 'fine art' works executed in fabric. In this field, the tendency over the last few years has been for a greater three-dimensional quality, and in present day exhibitions of embroidery and fabric collage panels, padding and quilting techniques are much in evidence. Quilting has also been used by some American artists who normally work in paint or print, furthering the present tendency to break down the barriers between one art form and another.

7   *Many Moons*   Quilt, (203 cm ×
224 cm: 80 in. × 88 in.) incorporating
twenty four small landscapes in
transparent appliqué. The piece is hand
quilted and reversible   Joan Schulze

8   Panel combining print, appliqué and
quilting   Vivienne Worral

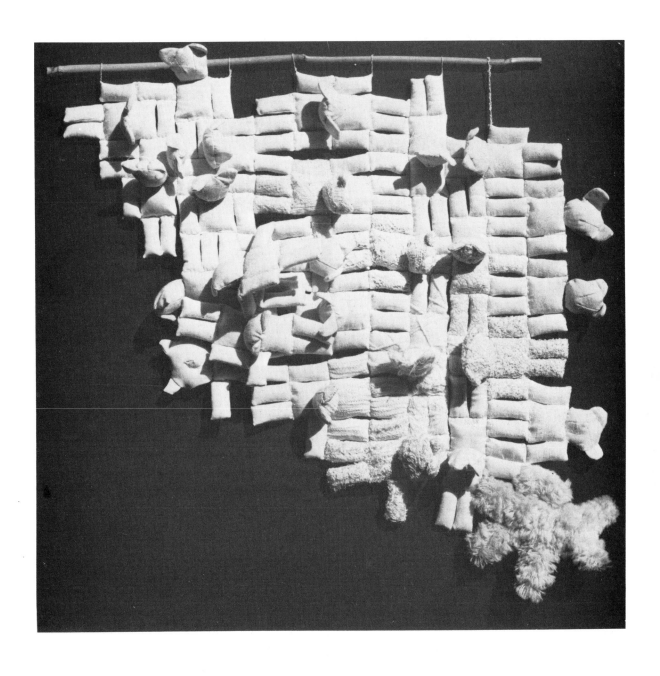

9 *opposite* Section of man's cap, (18th century) showing quilting and pulled work combined   Victoria and Albert Museum, Crown copyright

10   *Teddy Bears* Hanging   Anne Gillespie

11   *Riding the waves*   Eirian Short

12 Heraldic Swan making a wall
decoration in a bathroom. The use
of PVC which can be sponged down
makes the large areas of white
practicable   Eirian Short

Wadded quilting

also known as English Quilting

construction Three layers — top fabric, filling and backing held together by all over stitching (figure 13).

purpose To give extra warmth; to cushion against hardness; to enliven surface texture.

materials *Top fabric* any smooth, closely woven fabric such as cotton, fine linen, silk; light leather, suede, chamois. Materials made from man-made fibres do not quilt as well as natural ones, being too springy. Light tones show up the quilting more effectively than dark ones; matt or shiny surfaces are a matter of personal preference.

Filling for slight padding use fluffy domette (a loosely knitted cotton fabric); one layer or more of a soft fabric such as flannel or foam-backed jersey (this is good because it does not move about during the quilting process).

For greater padding use synthetic wadding, which comes in several thicknesses.

Backing when the backing will be seen (as in a bed cover) use the same material as top fabric, or a cheaper version of it. When the backing is hidden (as in a lined garment) use quilting muslin, butter muslin (cheesecloth), organdie or mull.

threads Match to top fabric, ie silk on silk, cotton on cotton. On cotton use a 40 or 50 cotton or buttonhole twist. The colour should match the top fabric, but can be in a darker tone.

stitches *By hand* running stitch, back stitch, chain stitch, pearl (figure 160).
By machine straight stitching, satin stitch, automatic stitches or free running.
The stitching should be distributed over the whole surface of the work in order to hold the three layers of material together.

design Much of the character of traditional quilting design springs directly from the purpose of the stitches. Thus, in wadded quilting, where the function of the stitches is to hold together three layers of

Facing Two views of a simply quilted, reversible jacket (46 cm × 36 cm: 18 in. × 14 in.) for a child, by Evie Edwards

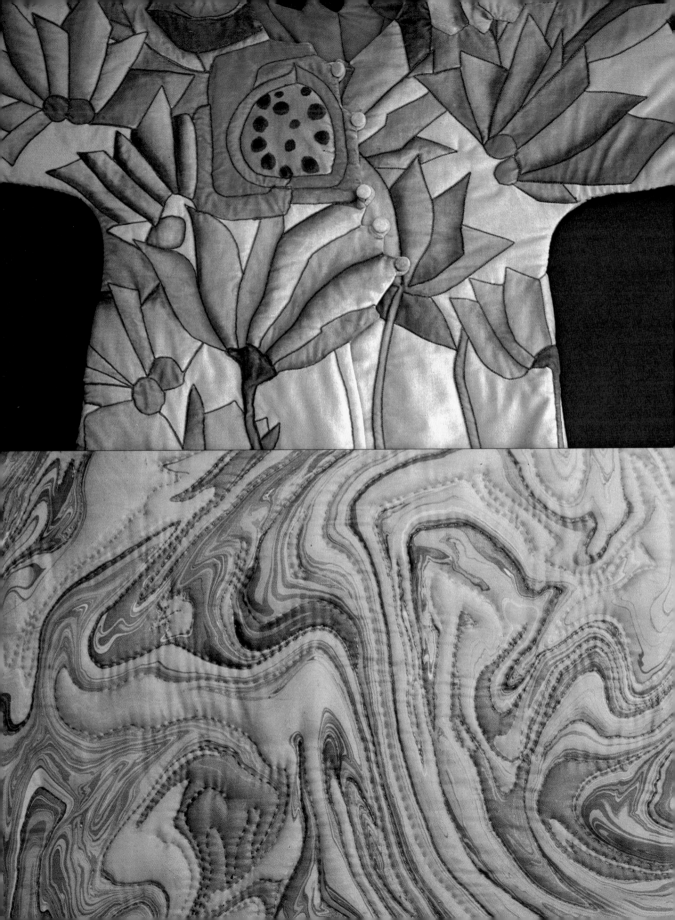

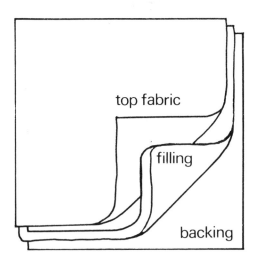

13　Construction for wadded quilting: top fabric, filling and backing

14　Non-repeating all-over pattern from natural source (magnified cross section of lichen)

material, it is logical to find the pattern evenly distributed over the whole area to be quilted. Big areas devoid of stitching would allow the layers to move in relation to each other, so all-over patterns are appropriate. It also seems reasonable to deduce that stitching which follows the warp and weft of the fabric will not give as great a strength as stitching done diagonally or in circular fashion. A look at historical quilting will indeed show that the diamond (crossed diagonal lines) and the spiral are amongst the most ancient and often used patterns. Bearing in mind, therefore, the purpose of the stitching, suitable designs for wadded quilting fall into three main categories. 1　all over repeating patterns. 2　all over non-repeating patterns. 3　patterns designed to fill a specific area.

Facing (above)　Detail of velveteen evening coat by Joy Stocksdale, quilted on the machine in cable stitch, then painted with acrylic paints
Facing (below)　Hand quilting in running stitch on a printed fabric with marbled pattern. See also photograph on page 94

1 All over repeating patterns

The basis of all over repeating patterns may be geometric shapes (ie straight lines, circles, squares, triangles, hexagons, etc) or organic shapes (ie those found in nature) or shapes based on man made objects (eg machinery, architecture).

The simplest geometric repeat is the stripe. From a basic regularly repeating stripe ideas can be developed by, for instance, varying the spaces between the lines, by turning the lines through 45 degrees or 90 degrees, or by making the stripes wavy or angular (figure 15a–g). Figure 16 shows the square repeated in straight lines horizontally and vertically; in a half drop; overlapping; turned through 45 degrees and in a chequerboard arrangement. These permutations can be tried with other enclosed geometric shapes. Overlapping circles, for instance, create the satisfying traditional pattern known as the 'wineglass' (or in America 'teacup') design (figure 75). For this kind of design an actual glass or cup may act as a template, round which to draw, but metal and plastic templates can be bought in a variety of shapes and sizes. Figure 19 shows a number of possible arrangements of the shell template, which although it carries an organic name, is in fact mathematically constructed from a half circle and two quarter circles. Individually designed templates may be cut from card provided strict accuracy is observed in their construction, as a small error in a template will cause considerable distortion when multiplied many times over a large area. It is not necessary to keep to one shape throughout a design. Figure 17 shows a design combining several geometric shapes, while in figure 18 geometric and organic shapes are combined.

When natural forms and man made objects are used as units for repeats they may need to be simplified or abstracted to fit in with the formal character of the repeat (figure 21). Some thought should also be given to the shapes made by the ground between the juxtaposed motifs (figure 23).

g

15　All over repeating patterns based
on the stripe
(a) vertical (b) vertical and horizontal

(c) diagonal (d) chequer board (e)
chevron (f) diamond (g) curves
forming, left to right, waves, ogees and
cables

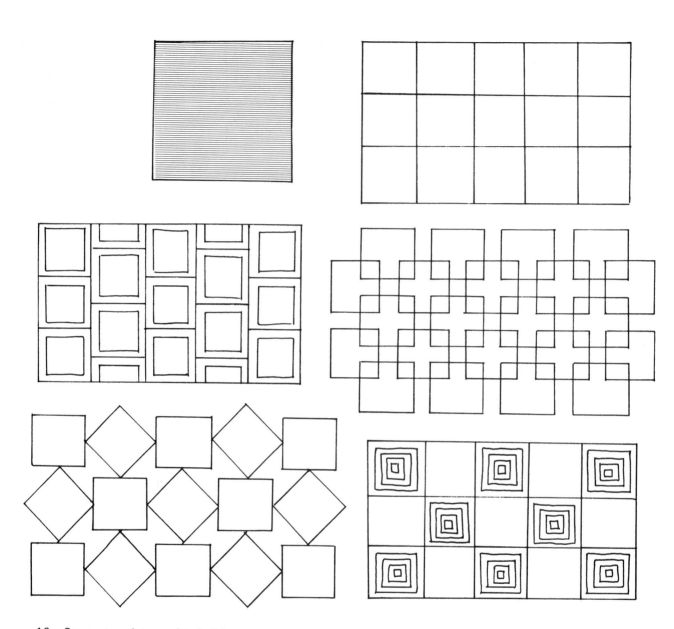

16 Square template used to build up
all-over repeating patterns

17 All over repeating pattern using a variety of geometric shapes

18 A combination of geometric and organic shapes

29

19 Designs based on the shell template

20 *opposite* Panel Pat Hopcraft

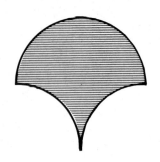

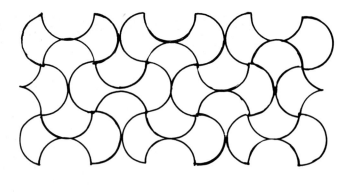

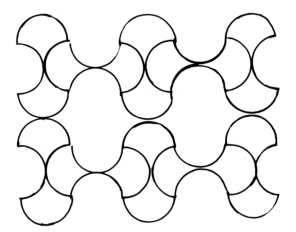

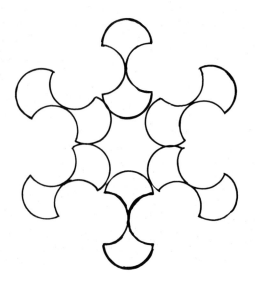

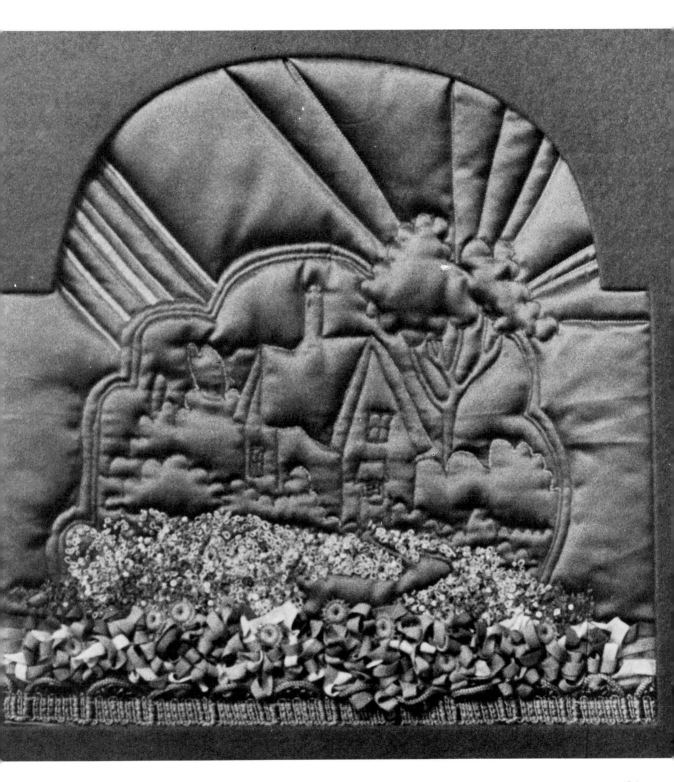

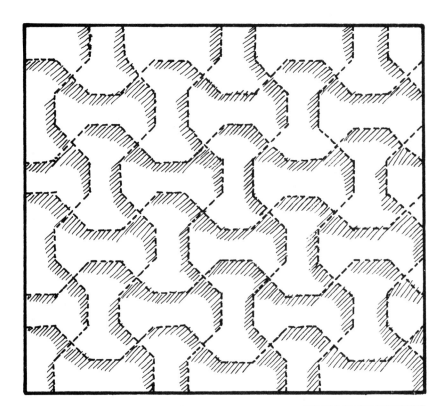

21 All over design based
on cotton reels

22 Leaf shapes design
to fit together in
a close all over pattern

32

23 Shoe motif turned over horizontally
and vertically. When used in an all over
design the spaces between the motifs
take on an importance equal to that of
the motifs

2 Non repeating all over patterns

All over patterns need not necessarily repeat in a regular sequence. A simple geometric or organic shape could, for instance be scattered at random and in varying sizes over an area (figure 25). More complex patterns may be found in nature, such as tree bark, animal markings, and the surface of water. These can be simplified and adapted for quilting (figures 14 and 26). Other random patterns can be created by dribbling paint, taking rubbings, crumpling paper and opening it out, etc. Patterns taken directly from nature will have an inborn feeling of unity, but in composing a design of scattered motifs it is important that some sort of 'family likeness' is maintained between the various elements in the design. In this way a 'busy' or disjointed design can be avoided.

24 Non repeating all over pattern based on geometric shapes

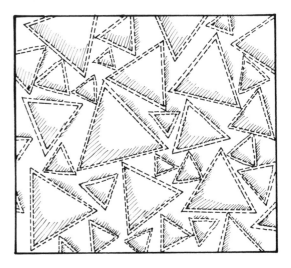

25 Random scattering of triangles of varying size

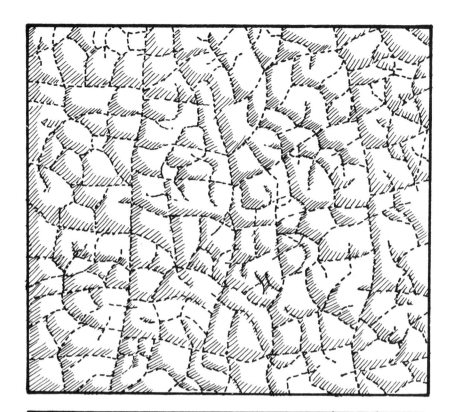

26 Non repeating all over pattern taken from nature – part of a skeleton leaf

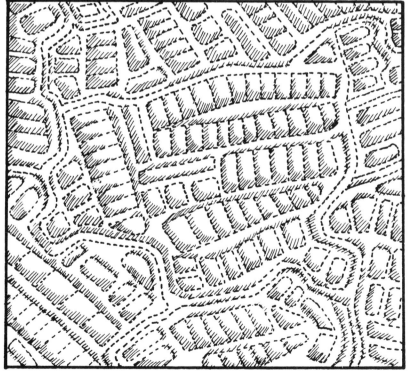

27 Man-made pattern – aerial view of a trout farm

35

3 Patterns designed to fill a given space

All over patterns, whether repeating or non repeating, by their very nature lack a focal point and could therefore become tedious when used over too large an area. Traditionally, large objects such as bed quilts have designs which specifically fit the rectangular or square shape and have definite points of interest. Figure 28 shows a typical Welsh quilt design with a central motif and borders. Others have one main motif, several subsidiary points of interest with the spaces in between filled by a smaller repeating pattern. The present day quilter may want to break with tradition and use, say, a more pictorial design, but consideration should still be given to having definite points of interest, and contrasts of scale and texture. Traditional templates, and the way they were used to build up rich and varied patterns are described in detail by Averil Colby in *Quilting*, Batsford, 1972.

The same principles apply to designing quilting for clothes. Many examples are given in the chapter on clothes and accessories.

28 Building up a design to fill a specific space. The central motif and border layout are typical of many Welsh quilts

36

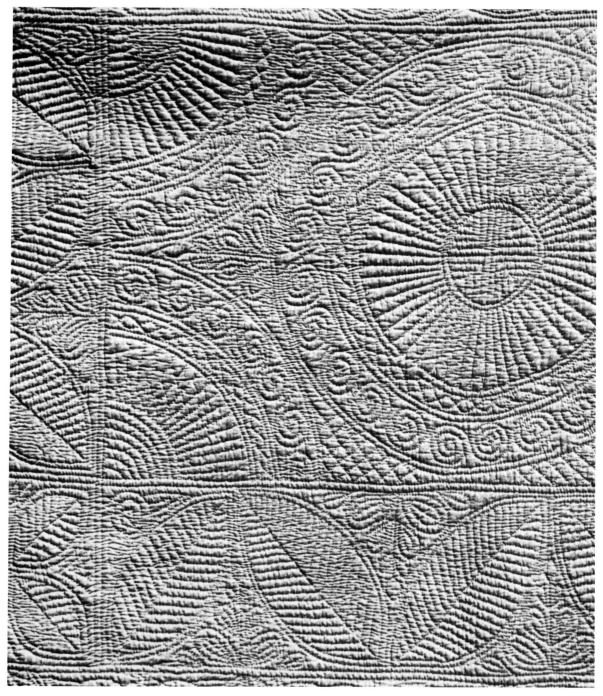

29   Detail of Welsh quilt, circa 1890

method

1 Iron top fabric and backing.

2 Mark on design if paint or crayon is being used. Other, less permanent methods of marking are best left until later (see page 148).

3 Tack all layers together, thoroughly smoothing the fabrics while sewing. For small pieces tack out from centre; for larger ones, in a horizontal and vertical grid (see page 144).

If the work is being framed for quilting stretch backing on frame, smooth out filling and top fabric and tack through all three on frame. If a frame is not being used spread out layers on a table or on the floor. Never skimp on the tacking, as adequate tacking will prevent 'riding' of the materials during work.

4 Mark designs which are to be chalked or needlemarked. Only mark as much as you can work at one sitting as this type of marking rubs off with handling. When machining simple geometric repeats it is often enough to mark only the first line in any direction (see figure 33).

5 Carry out stitching by hand or machine.

6 Remove tacking.

7 Finish in one of the ways shown in figure 34. Remember that the work will 'shrink' during the quilting process, so always allow for this when cutting out materials.

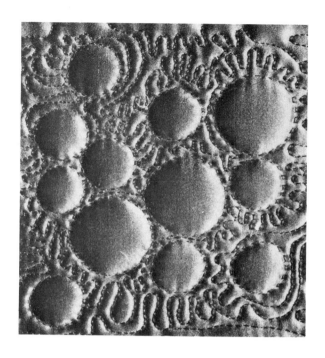

30 *opposite left*   Motif in wadded quilting worked by hand in running stitch   Sue Jenner

31 *opposite right*   Initial letter U worked in free running on the sewing machine

32 *left*   Wadded quilting, hand stitched in back stitch. Note how the plain areas stand out in strong relief from the closely quilted background. Ingrid Rowling.

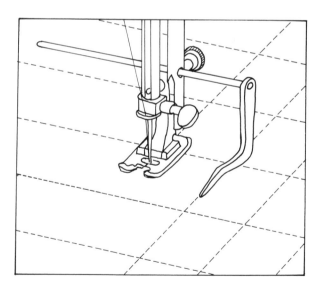

33   Using the gauge or edge marker to space out lines of stitching

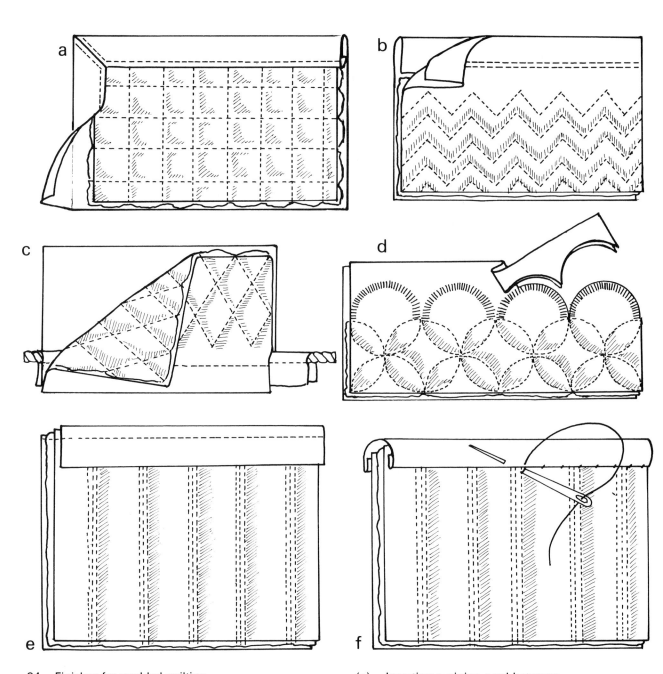

34   Finishes for wadded quilting

(a)   Bringing the backing over on to
the front of the work and machining it down

(b)   Turning in the top fabric and
backing and machining them together

(c)   Inserting a piping cord between
backing and top fabric

(d)   Working scallops and trimming
away surplus material

(e) and (f)   Binding

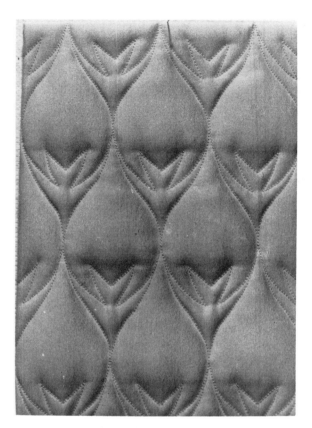

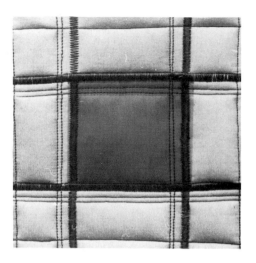

36 Appliqué and quilting carried out
in one operation using satin stitch on
the machine

35 All over repeating pattern based on
the ogee, worked in wadded quilting by
Sister Helen McGing. The padded effect
has been heightened by spraying with
dye after the stitching was completed

37　Welsh quilt lined with nineteenth
century cotton print, said to have been
made in 1770

38 Quilted and sprayed design in high
relief Ingrid Rowling

39, 40 Two roughs from a series
produced by experimenting with mixed
techniques. Colour has been flooded
on to the fabric with *Procion* dyes,
and quilting and embroidery worked
on the machine. One piece includes
an applied strip of machine knitting
Karen Nicol

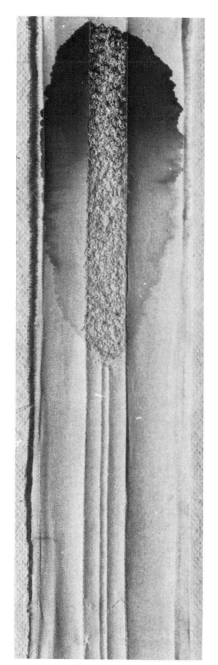

41, 42 Design for a bed quilt. The detail shows part of the design carried out in Fine Art Transfer Crayons, with machine quilting   Anita Eastwood

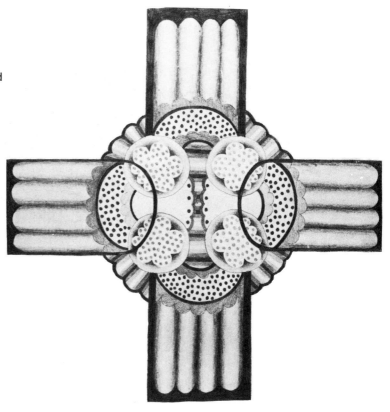

tied quilting

Wadded quilting can be tied instead of stitched. The work is prepared as for ordinary wadded quilting, but must be framed. Instead of the layers being joined with lines of stitching they are secured at spaced-out points by a knot. Use a strong thread – buttonhole twist, coton à broder, pearl cotton or a linen thread would be suitable.

method Tack layers of fabric together in a frame. Bring thread through fabric from the back leaving an end of about 50 mm (2 in.). Work two small stitches on the same spot, taking the end through to back of work and tying it with the end already there with two or three firm knots (figure 44). Trim off ends close to knot.

variations A bead or button can be attached while making the second small stitch (figure 45); or the tying can be done on the right side of the work, the ends being left slightly longer and tied into a small decorative bow (figure 46).

43   Tied quilting
Left: knot only
Right: knot with bead

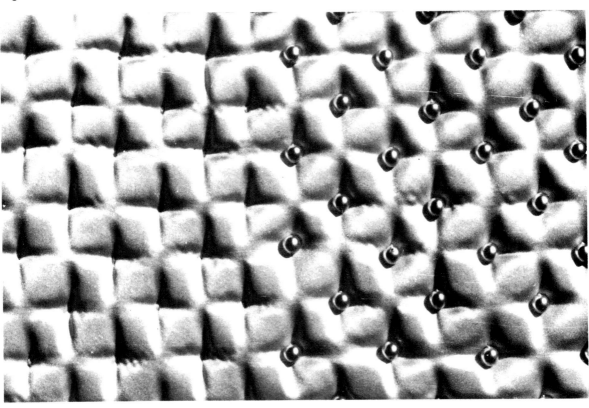

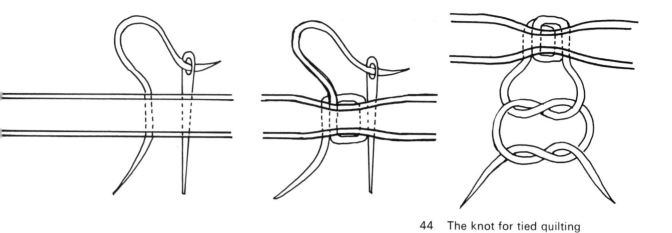

44   The knot for tied quilting

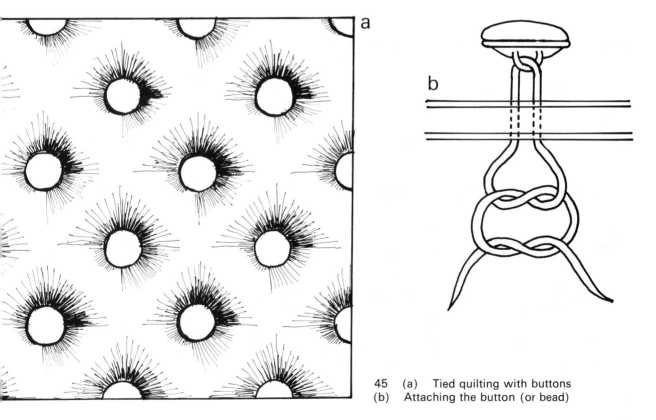

45   (a)   Tied quilting with buttons
      (b)   Attaching the button (or bead)

46 Tied quilting on stretch velvet

48 *Facing Cows grazing Among the Milky Way* (153 cm × 107 cm: 60 in. × 42 in.) Jody Klein. The decoration is airbrushed and rubber stamped on cotton. Hand and machine quilting are used. See also photograph on page 53

Overleaf Bumpy Quilt (114 cm × 153 cm × 18 cm: 45 in. × 60 in. × 7 in.) Jody Klein. Dyed cotton and cotton velvet. Individual sections were made up, stuffed, then joined together

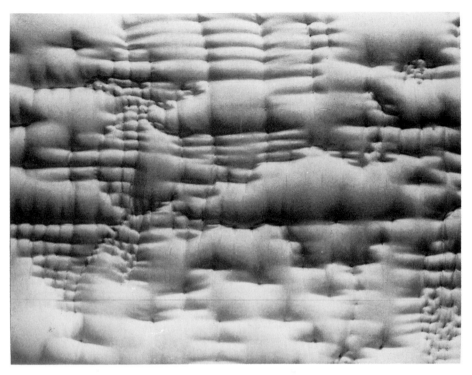

47 Free interpretation of tied quilting on Jap silk

48 Tied quilting on a hand knitted fabric

lap quilting

In most present-day homes a frame for setting up a bed quilt is too big to be practical, but large projects can nevertheless be undertaken by 'lap quilting', ie stitching the work in sections, putting the pieces together when the quilting is done. This method is also helpful with machine quilting as a double bed quilt is very cumbersome to manipulate on the machine.

construction   Blocks of wadded quilting joined together.

purpose   To carry out large projects in a confined space, or to facilitate handling on the machine.

materials   As for wadded quilting, allowing plenty for the extra seaming involved.

designs   The design must be planned to divide naturally into four, six or eight sections, or into strips. These are known as *blocks*.

method   Work each block as for ordinary wadded quilting, allowing ample material for turnings on top fabric and backing (figure 49a). When the quilting is completed trim the filler in each block to the exact size required, then lay two blocks face to face on each other and seam up the top fabric close to edge of filler (figure 49b); Open out (figure 49c). Repeat with two more blocks until the whole of the top is joined into one piece. Trim surplus material from seams. Turn over work and join up the backing. If the backing will be on view, as in a two sided quilt, this joining must be done neatly by turning in edges and slipstitching or oversewing them together (figure 49d). Tapes can be stitched over the seams to camouflage them and make an attractive criss cross pattern. The joins on the top side can be concealed by working one or two rows of quilting along them after the joining up is completed.

The waistcoat by Eve Lindsay (figure 50) was worked in eight pieces which were afterwards joined.

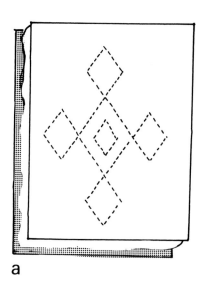

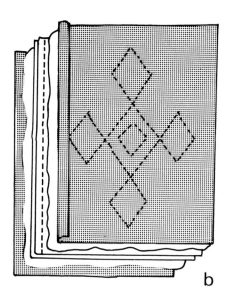

a

b

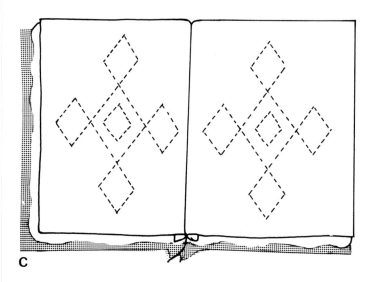

c

49 Lap quilting. Joining the completed blocks together
(a)   A completed block
(b)   Two blocks seamed together, face to face
(c)   The blocks opened out
(d)   The back neatened

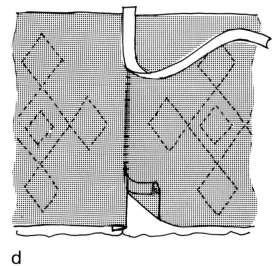

d

Flat quilting

construction *Two layers* top fabric and backing, held together by all over stitching (figure 52).

purpose To add weight to a flimsy fabric; to give protection at a point of hard wear (eg on the cuffs or pockets of a garment); to give a little extra warmth, without bulk, or to enliven large plain areas of 'background' fabric between scattered embroidered motifs.

materials *Top fabric* any smooth closely woven fabric (as for wadded quilting).
Backing as top fabric, or cheaper version of the same; muslin, organdie, or, if greater stiffness is required, a non-woven interlining.
For a reversible garment two layers of foam backed fabric in contrasting colours could be used, back to back.

threads Match to top fabric (ie cotton on cotton, etc).

stitches *By hand* any line stitch (back, running, chain stem, etc).
By machine as there is little undulation in the fabric in flat quilting, straight machine stitching looks a little thin, so a satin stitch, automatic embroidery stitch or cable stitch may be worked. Cable stitch is worked by threading the spool with a thicker thread than normal (perlé cotton is ideal), loosening the bottom tension to allow the thread to feed out easily and working with wrong side of the work uppermost. When the work is turned over the stitch on the right side has the appearance of a next line of couching.

designs Any fairly evenly distributed linear design.

method 1 Iron top fabric and backing.
2 Mark on design (see pages 146 and 147).
3 Tack fabric and backing together, right sides outwards (see page 144).

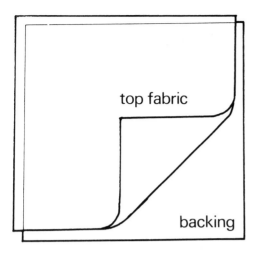

top fabric

backing

52   Construction for flat quilting: top
fabric and backing

53   Flat quilting using back stitches in
varying lengths

54   Flat quilting on an 18th century
pillow cover   Victoria and Albert
Museum, Crown copyright

55 Panel with quilted areas Julia
Graham Rogers

Corded quilting

also known as 'Italian' quilting

construction Two layers of fabric with cord insertion (figure 56).

purpose Mainly decoration, although the cording does add extra weight to a flimsy fabric. Sometimes in combination with stuffed quilting the background is solidly corded, giving real warmth and weight (figure 63).

materials *Top fabric*   any smooth, closely woven fabric, soft leather, suede, chamois and, handled with care, PVC.
Backing   butter muslin (cheesecloth), linen scrim or any soft, loosely woven fabric.
Insertion   cotton cord, such as piping cord or candlewick; rug wool; or, for softer effects, Italian quilting wool or knitting wool of appropriate thickness.

threads Match to top fabric (ie cotton on cotton, etc).

stitches Back stitch or straight machine stitching.

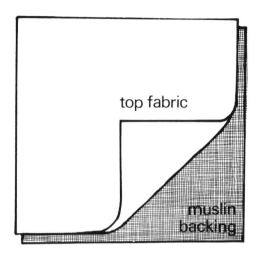

56　Construction for corded quilting:
top fabric with muslin backing

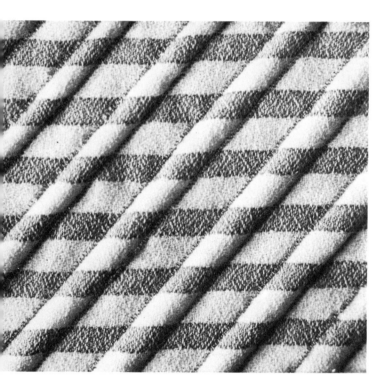

57　Corded quilting. Diagonal cording
on striped fabric　Sister Agnes Bernard

58　Simple geometric design in corded
quilting on red PVC　Ann Newman

designs In corded quilting the design is likely to be largely dictated by the technique. Although small isolated motifs are sometimes seen, they are tedious to work and it is more functional to compose a pattern of long continuous lines. Interlacing patterns are particularly satisfactory as the crossing over and under of the lines adds interest to the design, while still allowing the cording to be carried out with a long continuous filling thread. Inspiration for interlacing designs may be found, for example, in illuminated manuscripts, in mediaeval woodcarvings, on Islamic buildings, and in decorative knotting.

Original designs can be created by pinning out piping cord or any firm thread on a piece of soft board or an ironing table. By trial and error a satisfactory arrangement can be arrived at, which because it has been formed with cord, is bound to be suitable for carrying out in corded quilting. The satisfactory design can then be drawn up and transferred to the fabric.

Corded quilting can also be worked in a solid design, which is good when weight or warmth is needed as well as decoration. When quilting is being done on the machine solid cording has the advantage over wadded quilting that it is more manoeuverable on the machine, all the filling being inserted after the stitching is complete. This can be a great advantage in something as large as a bed cover.

Solid cording is particularly effective when used as a background to isolated stuffed motifs, as it throws them into greater relief. This combination is often found on American quilts.

Cording is also useful for outlining or emphasising shapes as in the 'Q' in the frontispiece.

59   Three lines of continuous corded quilting form this motif suggestive of sailor's knotting

60

60 *opposite* All over repeating pattern in corded quilting based on a Hardanger embroidery technique

61 *above* Interlacing border designs from classical sources, suitable for corded quilting

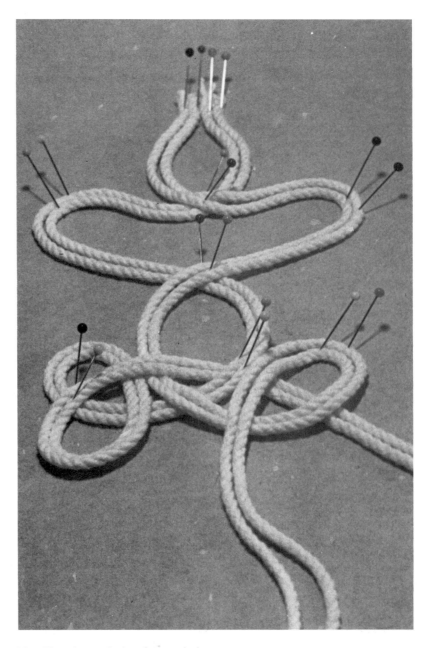

62   Planning a design for corded
quilting by pinning piping cord on soft
board

63   Stuffed motif standing out from a background of solid cording

64 and 65   Two examples of corded quilting used for gathering material where fullness is required

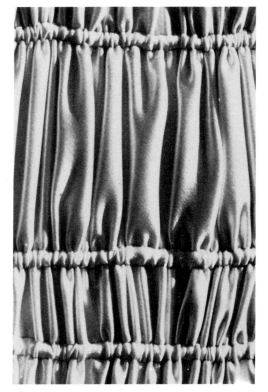

method
1 Iron top fabric well.

2 Spread out backing and place top fabric, face uppermost on it. Tack together thoroughly (see page 144).

3 Transfer design to top fabric by any of the methods explained on page 146. Make sure all lines are double.

4 Carry out stitching by hand (back stitch) or machine (straight stitch).

5 Take out tacking.

6 Turn work over. Select thread which, when inserted, will comfortably fill the space between the parallel lines of stitching. Thread into tapestry needle or rug needle (depending on its thickness).

Insert the needle into the backing, between two lines of stitching, making sure that the needle does not pierce the top fabric. Push needle along, drawing thread between lines. Whenever a strong curve or sharp angle in the line is reached bring the needle out and reinsert it at the same point, leaving a small amount of cord projecting each time (figure 66). This prevents the work 'cockling'. Where lines of cording cross, bring the needle out on one side of the line to be crossed and insert it on the other side of the line.

Note if cotton cord is used for the filling it should be soaked in water first to shrink it, otherwise the first time the quilted article is washed distortion will occur. Dry it thoroughly before use.

7 Trim off all ends of cords to about 3 mm ($\frac{1}{8}$ in.). Corded quilting must be lined.

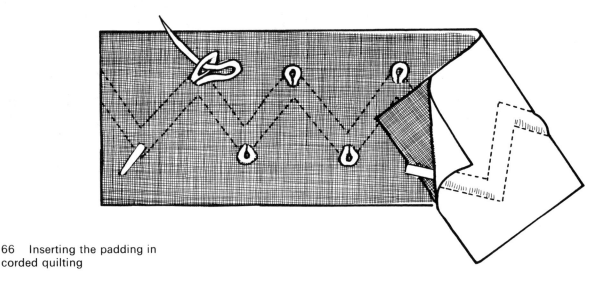

66 Inserting the padding in corded quilting

67 *Landscape* Phyllis Ross. The
landscape, in corded quilting, and the
padded frame, are calico. The trees are
embellished with french knots

68 *White Wall Quilt* Doris Hoover.
In white muslin and satin, quilted on the
machine with stuffed and corded areas
(137 cm × 153 cm: 54 in. × 60 in.)

69 *Moonscape* Doris Hoover. White
Muslin, satin and knitted fabrics, using
machine quilting, corded quilting and
stuffed quilting (122 cm × 153 cm:
48 in. × 60 in.). Owned by the
Counselling and Psychotherapy Center,
Palo Alto, California

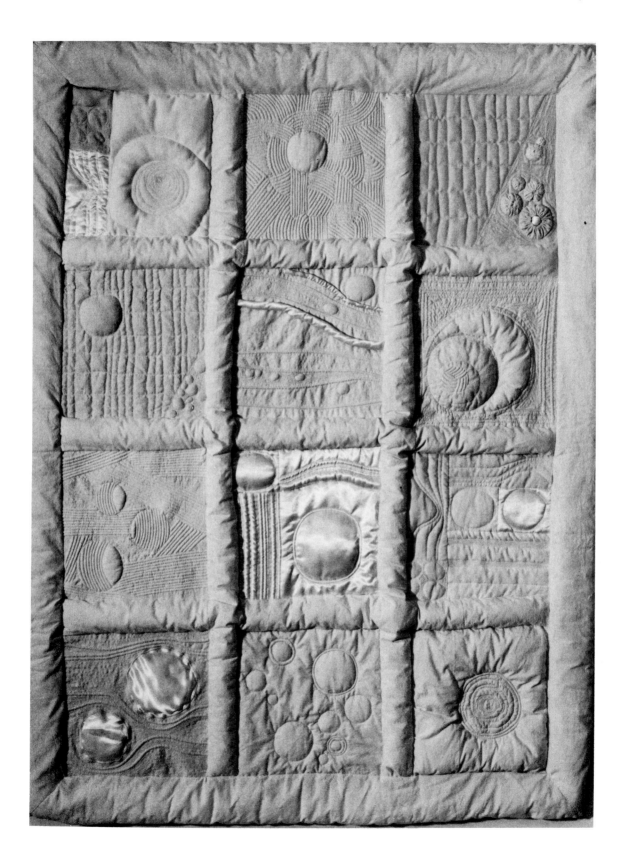

corded quilting on a single fabric

(a)   By hand, on a single layer of fabric

The appearance of corded quilting can be achieved on a single fabric by securing a cord to the underside of the fabric with a double back stitch. Use a firm cord, holding it in position under the fabric with the left hand, while working the double back stitch with the right hand on the upper side of the fabric (figure 70). Alternatively, the design can be traced on the back of the work and the stitching done from the back in a close herringbone. The effect on the right side is identical but the second method requires greater care in execution to produce neat lines of backstitching on the right side (figure 71).

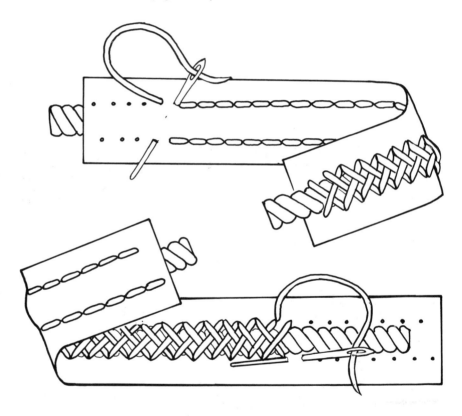

70 *top* Corded quilting on a single layer of fabric worked from the right side

71 *bottom* Cord attached to single layer of fabric working from the wrong side

(b)   By machine

Using a raised seam attachment, (figure 72) or simply by using twin needles and tightening the tension on the spool case (figures 121 and 122).

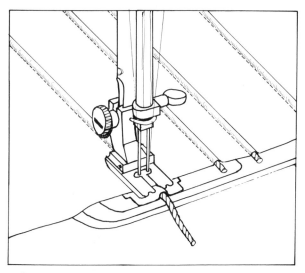

72   Using the raised seam attachment with twin needles

73   Fish, quilted and stuffed Jacqueline Ayling. The fish may be hung up as a decoration or used individually as cushions

Stuffed quilting

also known as Trapunto

construction *Two layers* top fabric and backing with some areas padded (figure 74).

purpose To give weight; to emphasise parts of a design.

materials *Top fabric* any smooth closely woven fabric, as for wadded and corded quilting.
Backing loosely woven muslin or linen scrim.
Filling wadding.

threads Match to top fabric (ie cotton on cotton, etc).

stitches *By hand* back stitch.
By machine free darning.

designs As with corded quilting the design is largely dictated by the technique, as stuffed quilting requires small enclosed shapes. Many of the larger motifs found on traditional quilts divide quite naturally into small enclosed areas, eg the American eagle with its formalised pattern of plumage, or the basket of fruit or cornucopia, with each piece of fruit separately stuffed. Figures 76 and 77 show many of the traditional motifs used in American quilts.

Some all over patterns are suitable for stuffing, eg the wineglass pattern. In figure 75 it is shown stuffed in four different ways, showing how the appearance of the design can be altered by emphasising different parts of the design.

Stuffed quilting combines well with corded quilting, making possible designs which balance linear and solid qualities (figure 81). It can also be used in combination with wadded quilting, to emphasise important parts of the design. Any stuffing done in this way is best worked first, through the top fabric and a muslin backing. Then, when the appropriate areas have been stuffed, an interlining and backing can be added and the whole thing worked as for normal wadded quilting. This emphasising of focal points in the design brings an added richness to wadded quilting.

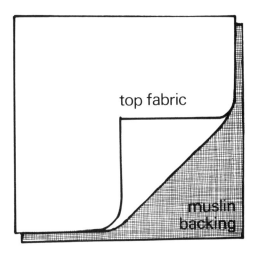

74 Construction for stuffed quilting:
top fabric and muslin backing

top fabric

muslin
backing

75 Traditional wineglass design stuffed
in four different ways, subtly changing
the emphasis in the pattern

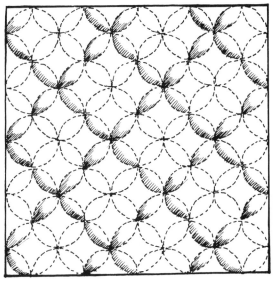

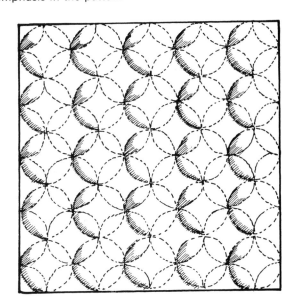

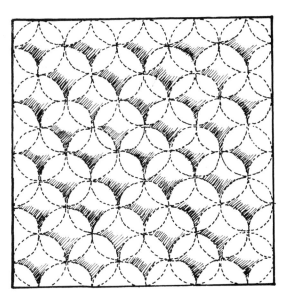

71

76 *Opposite* Stuffed motifs from American quilts, including the commonly found eagle and basket of fruit

77 *Below* This selection of stuffed motifs includes another version of the fruit basket and a cornucopia

method

1   Iron top fabric well.
2   Mark on design if using paint or crayon.
3   Spread out backing; place top fabric on it, face uppermost. Tack layers together thoroughly (see page 144).
4   Mark on design if it is being chalked or needlemarked.
5   Stitch round lines of design by hand or machine.
6   Take out tackings.
7   Turn work over.

For small shapes, pull a few threads of the backing aside and insert small pieces of torn off wadding, using a knitting needle or crochet hook to push the filling well into corners and points (figure 78b). Use enough filler to ensure that the shape stands out in relief on the front of the work.

Stroke muslin threads back into place.

For larger shapes, make a slit in the backing fabric, insert the stuffing and cobble up the slit with a few overcasting stitches (figures 78c and d).

8   All stuffed quilting should be lined.

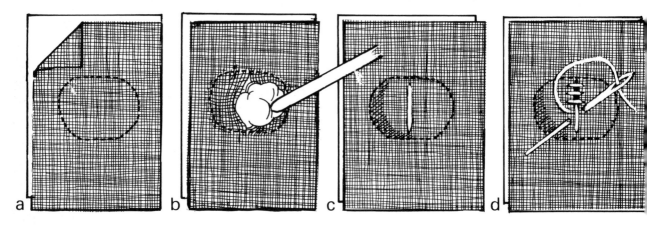

a   b   c   d

78   Inserting the filling for stuffed quilting
(a)   The back of the work with stitching complete
(b)   Parting the threads and pushing in wadding with a knitting needle
(c) and (d)   Alternative method: slitting the backing fabric to insert wadding

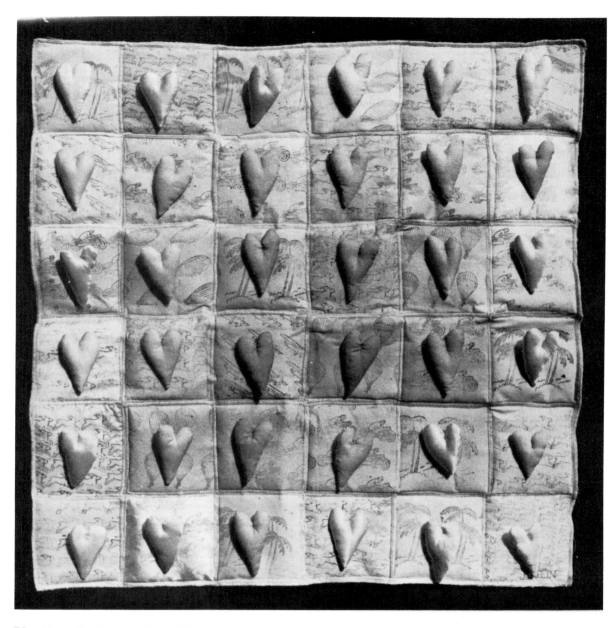

79 *Heart Quilt* Jody Klein. The
stuffed hearts in different pinks are
mounted on printed cotton squares.
The hearts are detachable to allow for
re-arrangement of the colours

80   Stuffed shapes with added french
knots   Ingrid Rowling

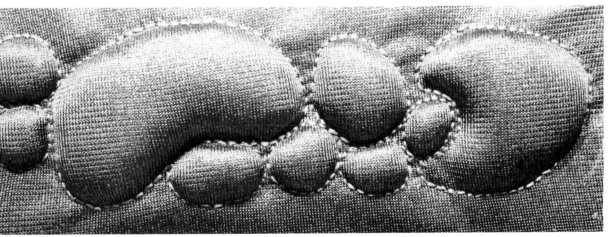

81 *above* Combination of flat, corded
and stuffed quilting   Sister Helen McGing

82 *below* Stuffed quilting worked on a
synthetic stretch fabric   Ingrid Rowling

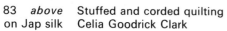

83 *above* Stuffed and corded quilting
on Jap silk Celia Goodrick Clark

84 *above right* Motif in stuffed
quilting Sister Helen McGing

85 *right* Free machine embroidery
on velvet with stuffed areas
Sue Jenner

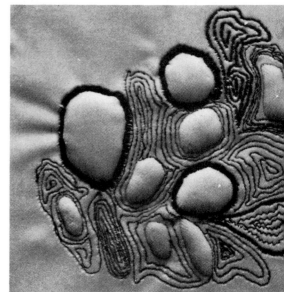

86 Detail of *We The People* a
bicentennial quilt (254 cm × 271 cm:
100 in. × 106 in.) Joan Schulze.
On each star is a soft sculpture face
using nylon stocking technique.
Appliqué is done by hand and both hand
and machine quilting are used. Owned
by the City of Palo Alto, California

Shadow quilting

construction	Two layers of transparent fabric with invisible filling (figure 88).
purpose	To bring delicacy and colour to what is normally a solid-looking monochromatic medium.
materials	*Top fabric* any transparent fabric such as organdie, voile, muslin, organza, fine silk or lawn. *Filling* embroidery or knitting wools in really strong colours (the colour is toned down considerably when seen through the top fabric), felt, beads, seeds, etc. *Backing* as top fabric.
threads	Match to top fabric (ie cotton on cotton, etc).
stitches	*By hand* back stitch. *By machine* straight stitching or free darning.
designs	Designs must consist of enclosed shapes and/or double lines, as in stuffed and corded quilting.

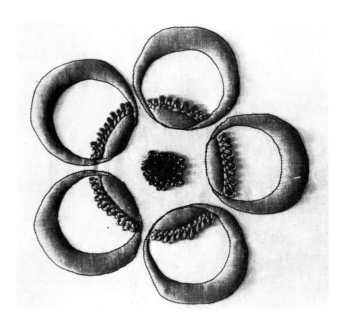

87   Shadow quilting worked on the
machine with additional hand
embroidery   Sister Helen McGing

80

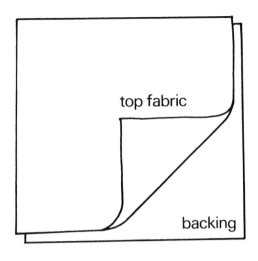

88 Construction for shadow quilting: two layers of transparent fabric

89 Shadow quilting in organdie over blue felt, with additional hand embroidery   Sister Agnes Bernard

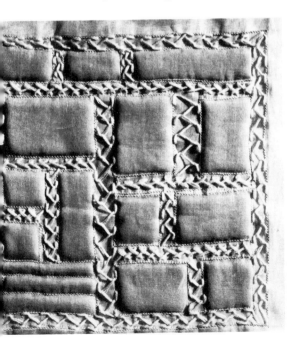

90 Motif in shadow quilting and hand embroidery. Both stuffed and corded quilting are used

method **(a)** **For corded and stuffed shadow quilting**

1 Iron fabrics.

2 Draw design out full size on paper. Place top fabric over the drawing and trace the lines of the design on with a white pencil or with poster colour and a really fine brush.

3 Put top fabric and backing together, right sides outward and tack thoroughly (see page 144).

4 Carry out stitching by hand or machine.

5 Turn work over. Insert fillings as for normal stuffed or corded quilting, but being careful with the cording not to leave too much of the wool projecting at curves and points or it will show through on to the right side of the work. In enclosed spaces use ends of knitting wool rather than wadding or for a sparkling effect insert beads, making sure that the slit through which they are inserted is sewn up firmly and neatly.

(b) **Padding with felt** For this type of work the design should consist of simple, flat areas of colour.

1 Lay backing fabric on a table wrong side uppermost. On this arrange felt shapes: do not let them touch each other, always allow enough room for a row or two of stitches in between (figure 91a).

2 Place top fabric right side uppermost over the arranged shapes and tack through all three layers, making sure that a line of tacking passes through each piece of felt (figure 91b).

3 Stitch round the felt shapes in backstitch or by machine.

4 Take out tacking (figure 91c).

91 Shadow quilting. Padding with felt shapes
(a) The felt pieces arranged on the backing

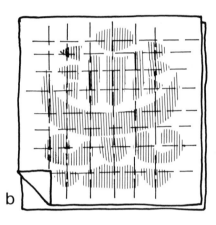

(b) The top fabric in place and all three layers tacked together

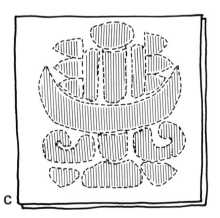

(c) The stitching completed and the tacking removed

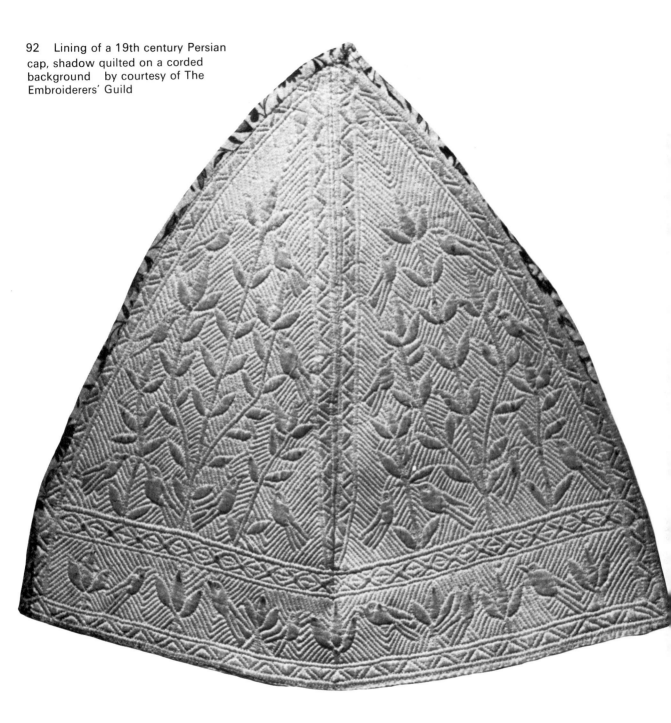

92   Lining of a 19th century Persian
cap, shadow quilted on a corded
background   by courtesy of The
Embroiderers' Guild

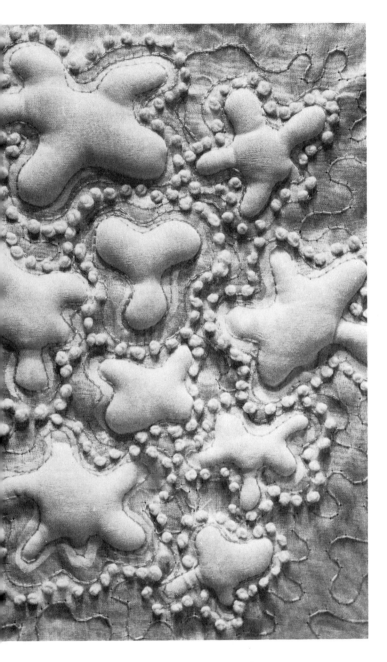

94   Interlacing lines of corded quilting
on white organdie. The lines are
threaded with red and orange coloured
wools   Sister Helen McGing

93   Stuffed shapes on white organdie
with additional stitching by hand and
machine

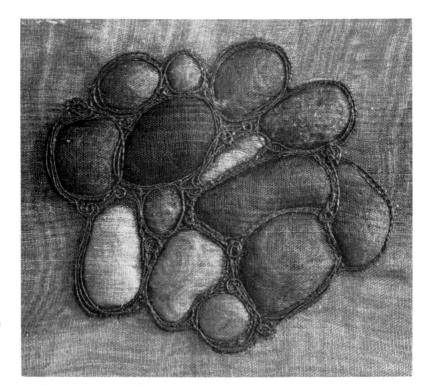

95 Shadow quilting worked in free running on the machine. Brightly coloured wools are inserted between two layers of shaded organza

96 Shadow quilting on organdie. Small silver beads replace the more usual wool filling

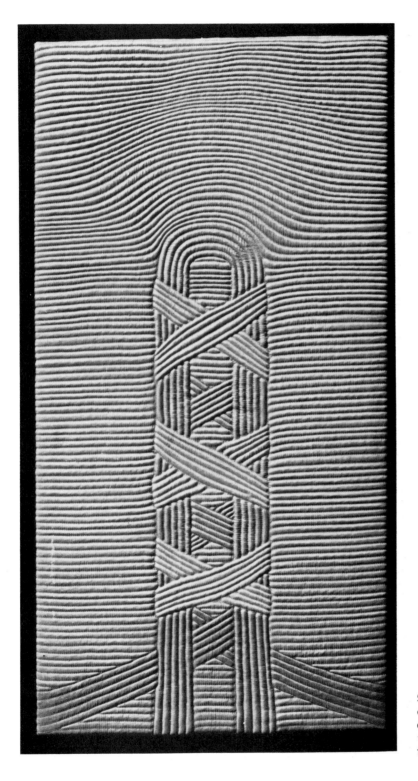

97 *Torus* Phyllis Ross. Solid cording on Jap silk. The wools for filling were dyed in carefully graded tones of grey which show subtly through the silk top fabric.

gathered quilting

construction Two layers of fabric, the top one gathered into a 'ruched' effect (figure 99).

purpose To give an interesting surface texture.

materials *Top fabric* this should be fairly stiff; a heavy satin gives a good effect, and even velvet can be used.
Backing same as top.

threads Match to top fabric (ie cotton on cotton, etc).

design Areas of gathered quilting must consist of enclosed shapes, but these can be combined with other types of quilting or incorporated into an appliqué design.

method 1 On right side of backing fabric mark the area to be filled with gathered quilting, say a circle, (figure 100a). From top fabric cut a similar shape but twice the size. Turn a small hem on to wrong side and secure with a row of running stitch (figure 100b). When running is complete draw up shape until it is the same size as that marked on to the background fabric.
2 Place it over the marked area and hem in place.
3 At this stage there should be a loose bag standing up from the background (figure 100c). Stab stitch at intervals over the applied patch and the fabric will fall into an interesting surface pattern (figure 100d).

98 and 99 Gathered quilting on velvet and satin

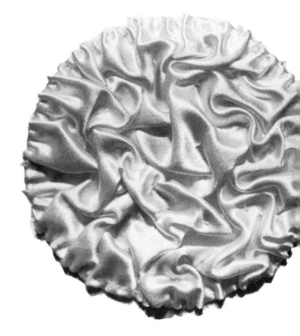

88

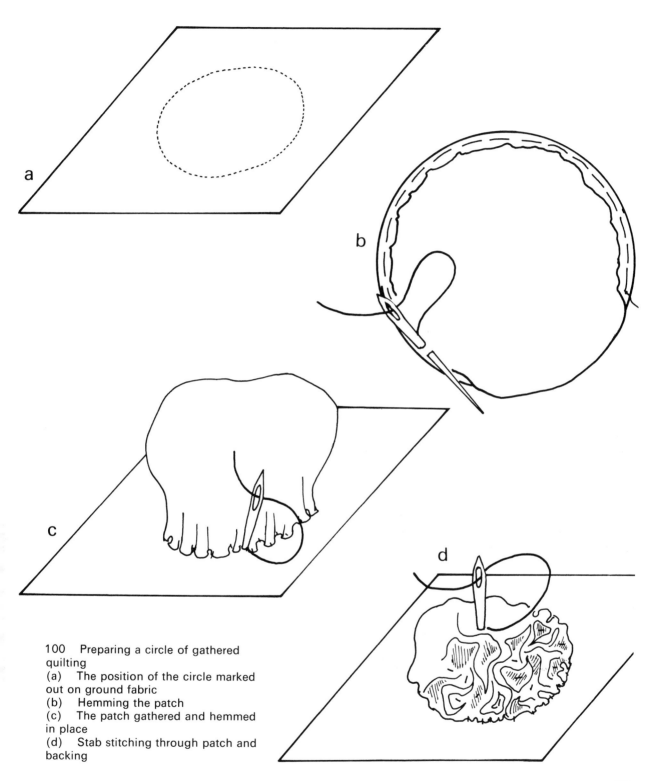

100 Preparing a circle of gathered
quilting
(a) The position of the circle marked
out on ground fabric
(b) Hemming the patch
(c) The patch gathered and hemmed
in place
(d) Stab stitching through patch and
backing

Quilting on patterned fabrics

Because much of the beauty of intricate quilting may be lost when the work is done on patterned fabric, plain materials are usually chosen. It is noticeable that in ready-quilted fabrics on the market, when printed fabrics are used the quilting is usually confined to a simple diamond pattern which does not relate to the print in any way. However, positive use can be made, in a number of ways, of patterned materials, both printed and woven. For instance, a rather static design of, say, stripes or checks can be enlivened by using quilting deliberately to distort the surface pattern. Conversely, the fabric can be enhanced and emphasised by actually using it as the basis for the quilting design. This technique is known as 'contour quilting', and can be carried out in wadded, stuffed or corded quilting, adapting the method to the character of the fabric design.

101 Gingham tucked, pleated and quilted   Anne Preston

102 Corded and wadded quilting on a
damask weave satin

quilting on striped fabric

The simplest example of contour quilting is the use of striped fabric for cording. Printed stripes may be the obvious choice, but in fact many woven fabrics could be used, providing the weave was not too loose. Delicate shadow effects can be obtained by using self stripe muslin or voile and threading with a coloured wool filler.

For contour quilting on stripes, follow the instructions for normal corded quilting, omitting the transferring of design, and stitching instead along the edges of the stripes. When the stripes are straight, it will not be necessary, when inserting the filler, to bring the needle out through the backing at any point along the stripe, but a short length of the filler cord should be left at the beginning and end of the line to allow for shrinkage.

Some or all of the stripes may be padded depending on the effect required. Solid cording will give greater weight and warmth if that is required. Experiments can be made with cording at right angles to, or diagonally across the stripes to break up the rigidity of the pattern (figures 103, 104).

103 and 104   Quilting used to distort stripes

contour quilting on scattered motifs

Fabrics which have spots or other self contained motifs 'powdered' over their surface lend themselves to stuffed quilting. Follow the instructions for stuffed quilting, outlining each spot or motif completely, by hand in backstitch or on the machine in free darning. The amount of stuffing inserted into each motif will depend on the weight of the fabric and the position of the motif on the garment or article. Motifs near the hem of a garment or curtain could be stuffed tightly to give weight and an impression of high relief, those near the top of the article being only slightly padded.

105 Isolated motifs contour quilted and stuffed, making them stand out in high relief

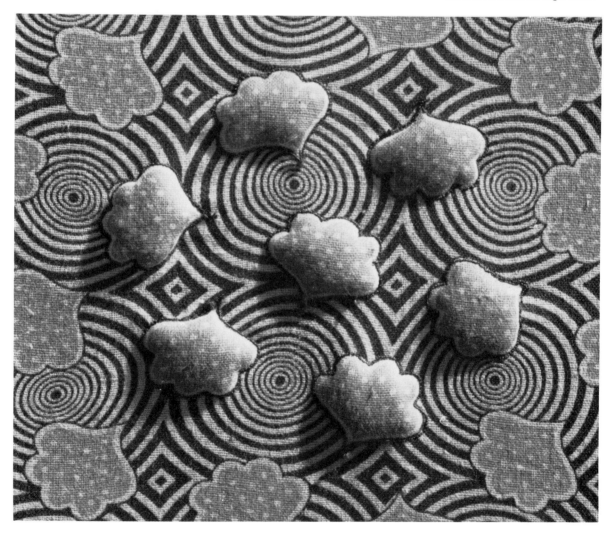

contour quilting on all over patterns

Prints of an 'all over' nature suggest the use of wadded quilting, which requires evenly distributed stitching to hold the layers together. If the design on the fabric is a simple one, follow the directions for normal wadded quilting, apart from transferring the design, and stitch round all components of the design. If, however, the design is a complex one (for instance a Paisley pattern) a certain amount of selection will be necessary. Slavishly quilting round every part of the design could result in finished work looking 'busy' and overworked. Aim at a balanced arrangement of stitched and plain areas (figure 106). Focal points in the design can be given extra emphasis by backing and stuffing them before the layers are assembled for the wadded quilting process (figure 107).

106   Hand quilting in running stitch on a printed fabric with marbled pattern. See also colour plate facing page 25

107 Contour quilting on antique silk fragment. Stuffed and wadded quilting are used.

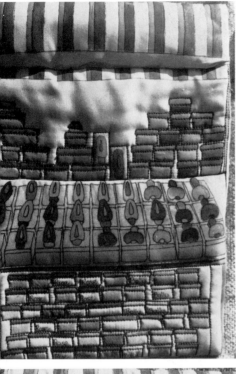

108 to 111 *Street Market* Pamela
Jeffrey. Four small panels which are
printed and then machine quilted

Simulated quilting

Whereas true quilting takes time and patience, there are a number of ways in which a quilted effect can be achieved by quicker means. It must be realised, however, that it is not possible to obtain by these methods the same variety and richness of texture as in real quilting.

pillow quilting

construction Miniature 'pillows' joined together (figure 112e).

purpose To combine patchwork with a quilted effect in one operation.

materials A mixture of colours or patterns and plains in like materials (ie all cottons, all wools, etc).
Filling pieces of synthetic wadding, foam chips.

threads Ordinary sewing thread for machining, buttonhole twist for oversewing or a fairly thick embroidery thread such as cotton perlé if faggotting is used to join the pieces.

stitches Straight stitching on the machine. Oversewing or faggotting by hand.

design An arrangement of squares and rectangles.

method 1 Prepare a number of square and/or rectangular pillows in the following way.
For each pillow cut two pieces of fabric the same size, allowing for seams. Place pieces face to face and machine round three sides (figure 112a).
Trim surplus material from corners and turn inside out. Fill with wadding or foam chips (figure 112b) and close opening with slip stitch or neat oversewing (figure 112c).
2 Arrange the prestuffed units to form a pleasing design.
3 Join together with oversewing on the wrong side, or by faggotting for a more decorative effect (figure 112d).

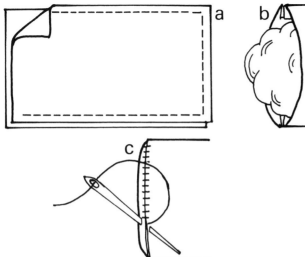

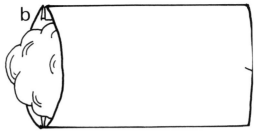

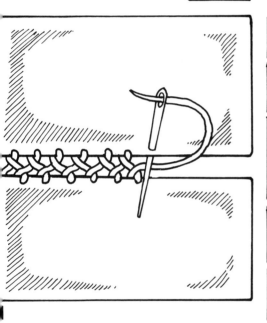

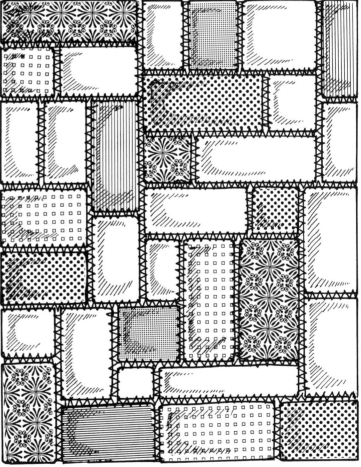

112   Pillow quilting
(a) (b) and (c)   Making up the pillow
(d)   Joining the pillows together with faggoting
(e)   The completed quilt

raised patchwork
also known as Swiss Patchwork

A variation on pillow quilting, but on a smaller scale and using traditional patchwork shapes.

construction Stuffed geometric patches joined together (figure 115).

purpose To produce an effect of patchwork and quilting in one operation.

materials Closely woven smooth fabrics for the patches. Wadding for filling.

threads Ordinary sewing cotton for machining.
A strong thread such as buttonhole twist for oversewing.

designs Arrangements of geometric units (triangles, hexagons, squares, etc).

method **(a)   For triangles**
1   Iron fabric.
2   Cut a number of squares of the same size (use a template for accuracy) (figure 113a).
3   Fold each square in half diagonally, with right side of fabric innermost. Seam up by hand or machine along one side and half way along the other side (figures 113b and c).
4   Trim corners and turn the patch right side out.
5   Stuff patch and close opening with neat oversewing (figures 113d and e).
6   When a number of patches have been prepared they can be arranged in a pleasing design and oversewn together firmly on the back (figure 113f).

(b)   For other geometric shapes   (eg hexagons) cut *two* pieces of fabric for each patch, lay them face to face and seam up, leaving an opening. Continue as for triangles.

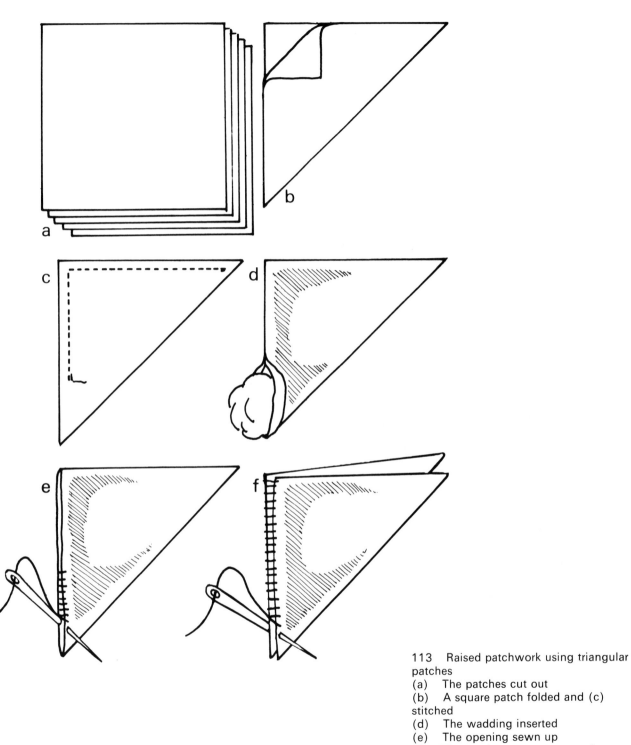

113   Raised patchwork using triangular patches
(a)   The patches cut out
(b)   A square patch folded and (c) stitched
(d)   The wadding inserted
(e)   The opening sewn up
(f)   The patches oversewn together

overlapping scales

This is another way of achieving an effect of patchwork and quilting in one operation.

construction Overlapping rows of padded 'scales' stitched to backing, (figure 117).

purpose To simulate patchwork and quilting quickly and easily.

materials An old sheet for backing.
Any closely woven smooth fabric for scales:
Plastic foam sheeting for filling.

threads Match to top fabric (ie cotton on cotton, etc).

designs Arrangements of plain and patterned scales, or scales in varying tones and colours.

method 1 Cut a template of the required size, in card, making the lower edge pointed or curved to choice (figure 118a).
2 Iron fabric, lay on table doubled, face to face.
3 Place template on top and chalk round it (figure 118b).
4 Seam up on chalked line round three sides, leaving the top open. Trim away surplus fabric leaving a little more at top of upper fabric (figure 118c).
5 Turn patch inside out and insert a piece of plastic foam cut exactly to size of template (figure 118d).
6 Turn top fabric over and pin scale to backing (figure 118e).
7 Repeat until there is a row of scales along entire width of backing, at the bottom.
8 Attach to backing with a line of machine stitching near the top of scales (figure 118f).
9 Attach the next row of scales above this, so that the line of stitching is hidden, and so on until the entire backing is covered (figure 118g).

117 Overlapping scales

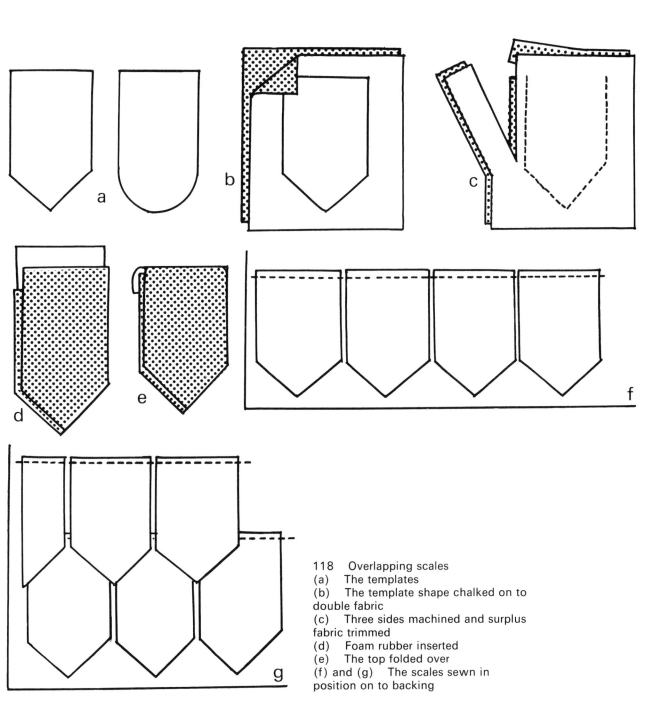

118 Overlapping scales
(a)   The templates
(b)   The template shape chalked on to double fabric
(c)   Three sides machined and surplus fabric trimmed
(d)   Foam rubber inserted
(e)   The top folded over
(f) and (g)   The scales sewn in position on to backing

suffolk puffs or yo-yo quilting

construction   Gathered circular patches sewn together (figure 119).

purpose   Purely decoration – eg on bedcovers, dress, etc.

materials   Fine, closely woven fabrics (cotton or silk) in a mixture of plain colours or prints. Small checks and stripes give interesting results.

threads   Strong cotton such as buttonhole twist or a strong silk.

designs   Arrangements of circular patches in horizontal and vertical rows.

method   1   Using card, make a round template just over twice the size of the required patch. Cut a number of fabric circles from it, and gather them up as follows.

2   With wrong side of patch facing upwards, turn a narrow hem on to the wrong side and secure with a running stitch (figure 120a).

3   When running is completed draw the patch up tightly and secure thread with a double stitch. Trim thread close to work. Spread gathers evenly and press lightly (figure 120b).

4   Join the patches together, gathered side uppermost, by overcasting with a few stitches on back of work. This slightly squares off the shape of the patch, but it is necessary to give sufficient strength to the resulting fabric. The patches may be joined in a straight repeat or in a half drop (figure 120c).

The joined patches can be mounted on to a backing fabric of contrasting colour, which would show through the holes. This obviously gives greater strength to the work.

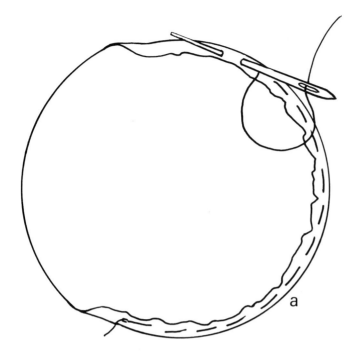

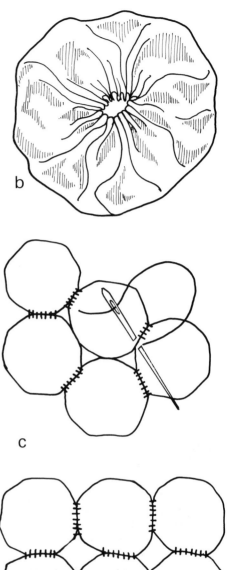

120   Suffolk Puffs
(a)   Turning in and gathering the patch
(b)   The completed patch, right side
(c)   Joining the patches with oversewing

119   *opposite*   Suffolk Puffs or Yo-Yos

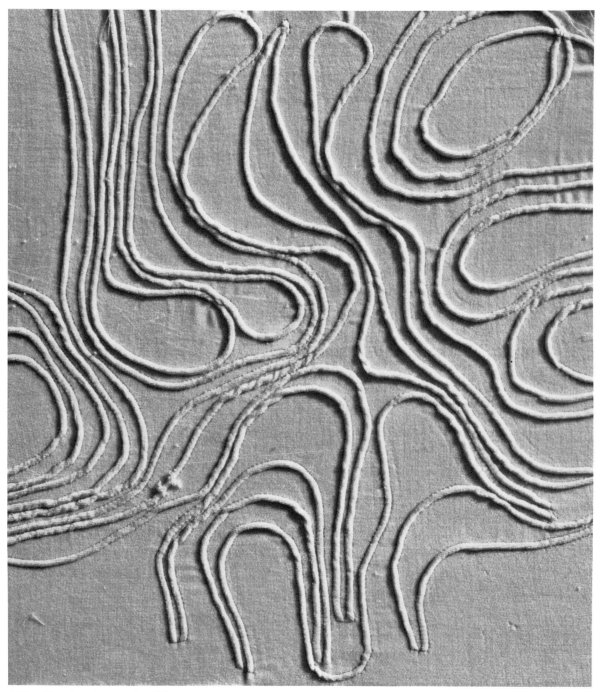

121 Simulated corded quilting on velvet. The effect is obtained by using twin needles and tightening the bottom thread tension

108

122 Simulated corded quilting on a self
stripe upholstery velvet

quilted effect with no stitching

Suitable only for panels and rigid constructions such as boxes, mirror frames, etc.

construction Two layers stuck together and with inserted shapes.

purpose To give an appearance of quilting without any stitching.

materials *Top fabric* any closely woven opaque fabric in a *natural* fibre (synthetics will not stand the heat necessary to iron the fabric down to the backing).
Filling cardboard, felt or plastic foam.
Backing iron-on interlining.

designs Simple geometric shapes not too small in scale are the easiest to handle with this method. Place them far enough apart to enable the toe of the iron to pass between them easily.

method 1 Place iron-on interlining sticky side uppermost on table.
2 Arrange cardboard, felt or foam shapes on it (use card for a hard edge effect, felt or foam for softer edges) (figure 124a).
3 Place top fabric face uppermost on top and, using the toe of the iron, press close up to the edges of the shapes, until the backing and top fabric are well stuck together (figure 124b).
4 Using the iron flat, press any large spaces in between motifs, making sure that the top fabric and backing are completely fused (figure 124c).

123 Simulated quilting with no stitching

a

124 Simulated quilting with no stitching
(a)   Iron on backing with cardboard shapes in place

b

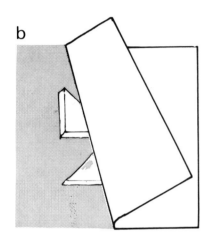

(b)   Top fabric placed in position

c

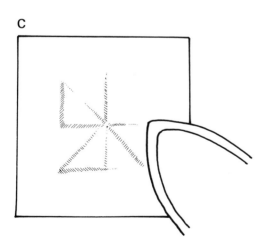

(c)   Press close to the edge of the card with the toe of the iron

Quilted clothes and accessories

Before embarking on quilted clothes or accessories it is a good idea to ask yourself *why* quilting has been chosen. The answer will, to a certain extent determine what type of quilting to use. If, for instance it is because warmth is required, as in a dressing gown, ski jacket or slippers, then wadded quilting would be the obvious choice. On the other hand, if the prime consideration is the need to reinforce the fabric against wear, as on cuffs, pocket flaps or belts, then flat quilting would be most suitable. Flat quilting could also be chosen if added weight were needed on a flimsy fabric, either all over the garment, or on details such as the yoke or hem. Corded quilting, on the other hand is used mainly for decoration, although *solid* cording is almost as warm as wadded quilting.

For the result to be successful it is essential that the chosen fabric, the style of the garment and the type of quilting should 'marry', eg the jacket in figure 136 is made of mattress ticking, a tough cotton fabric. The style has been kept uncomplicated and the quilting design is simple and designed in relation to the ticking stripes. The quilting is wadded, stitched by machine, through a heavy synthetic wadding. This would be much too cumbersome for, say, a silk dress where a more fluid look could be obtained by quilting through domette or even a soft fabric such as flannel. The design could affored to be finer and more intricate, worked in a silk thread, by hand or machine.

125 Designs for quilted jackets taken from fairground decoration Rozanne Hawksley

general hints

Whenever possible, pre-shrink materials to be quilted. Fabrics can be rolled in a damp towel or blanket to damp evenly and then ironed. Linings and bindings should be included and cotton cord, if used for corded quilting, should be washed before use.

Make use of leaflets which are to be found at the fabric counters in most large stores. These point out the special characteristics of difficult materials such as velvet or suede and give advice on how to avoid pitfalls. If there are no leaflets available ask the assistant if there are any points you should watch out for. For instance, the hand quilting on the suede pocket (figure 147) was made much easier by the use of a triangular pointed leather needle which pierced the skin easily at every stitch.

Keep the shape of garments as simple as possible. A look at ethnic clothes will show that it is possible, by using simple geometric areas of fabric, to build up clothes of great richness and beauty. The kimono is ideal for quilting as there are no curved arm holes or set-in sleeves — just a few straight edges to seam together. The simplicity of the style makes the kimono a suitable basis for a wide variety of designs (figure 152).

Geometric garments also have the advantage that they do not need precise fitting. It is quite difficult with a fitted garment to assess accurately how much extra fabric to allow for shrinkage during the quilting process.

Geometric garments are not the only ones which can be used. Trade patterns, chosen with care, can be successful. Avoid styles with fullness, pleats or gathers and keep quilting on sleeve heads and underarms to a minimum. Buy a pattern by a manufacturer whose patterns you have used before, as methods and even measurements can vary from one make to another. Trace the bought pattern on to plain, strong paper and design the quilting *in situ*. *Sellotape* any darts together so that the design lines up across them. Even better, make a toile, ie a 'mock-up' of the garment in mull, calico or even an old sheet. The quilting design can then be marked on to the material with chalk or pencil and the effect seen in the round. A pattern or design worked out on a flat piece of paper can often look quite different when seen in three dimensions. Bear in mind that the toile may have to be at least a size too large to allow for shrinkage during quilting. How much will depend on where the quilting is placed. If it is confined to collars, cuffs, pockets, etc, it will make very little difference, but if the body of the garment is to be heavily quilted, shrinkage must be allowed for

126 Three designs for detachable pockets, the ideas taken from Victorian crafts   Rozanne Hawksley

115

127 Suggestions for quilted details on
clothes   Rozanne Hawksley

making up a quilted garment

(a) Making up a garment with an all over quilted pattern
This may be made up from a bought length of ready quilted fabric or it may be your own design. If the latter, it is advisable to quilt the entire length of fabric before cutting out the garment. When quilting a length on the machine, stitch alternate lines in opposite directions (figure 164) to counteract the layers of material 'riding' on each other under the pressure of the machine foot. Also, use both hands to smooth the bulk of fabric outward and away from the foot as the fabric is fed through. Once the entire length of fabric is prepared, make up the garment in the usual way, but keeping the following points in mind:

1   You should have chosen a simple style of garment, but you may still have a set-in sleeve. As it is difficult to ease a bulky quilted sleevehead into an armhole, leave the sleeve seam and garment side seam open until after the sleeve head has been set in. Then any surplus fabric can be got rid of in the seams.

2   Do not cut out any of the pattern pieces with the fabric double, even if it is shown thus in the lay out. The bulkiness of the quilted fabric will cause distortion, so cut all pieces with the fabric opened out flat.

3   When the pattern pieces are cut and seam lines marked in, remove the filling from the seam allowance by unpicking the quilting to the seam line, trimming away the wadding. This will make for much neater seams. The same procedure can be carried out on darts, hems and openings.

4   Never turn up a double hem in quilted fabric. If the filling has not been removed, as explained above, bind the edge of the fabric and turn up a single hem.

(b) Using a quilted pattern designed for a specific garment
1   Choose a plain fabric for preference. Much of the detail of a carefully planned design could be lost on a busy printed material.

2   Make a toile or strong paper pattern and plan the quilting on this, so that it may be seen all round.

From here the procedure will depend on whether the quilting is being worked by hand or machine.

Machine quilting
1   Cut out all the pattern pieces three times — once in the top fabric, once in the filler and once in the backing. Allow a generous amount of extra material for shrinkage caused by the quilting process.

128 Machine quilted jacket in a mixture of small-scale printed cottons Jacqueline Ross

2 Prepare each pattern piece as for normal wadded quilting, marking on the design and tacking top fabric, filler and backing carefully together.

3 Stitch the design, stopping the stitching at the seam lines, to facilitate trimming of wadding from the seams.

4 Should the work have puckered up at all, this could be rectified at this stage by pinning each piece out tightly with drawing pins, (right side up) over a damp cloth or damp blotting paper and allowing it to dry.

5 Make up the garment in the normal way.

Hand quilting

1   Set up materials in a frame, as for wadded quilting. Trace tack round as many pattern pieces as will fit in to the frame at one time, eg two sleeves and a belt as in figure 153.

2   Mark out the design and carry out the quilting, stitching only up to the seam lines.

3   Remove fabric from frame and cut out pattern pieces. Repeat until all pattern pieces are prepared, then make up garment.

A garment need not be entirely quilted. Details such as quilted collars, cuffs, pockets or hems may be incorporated into an otherwise plain garment.

All the above instructions have been given as for wadded quilting, but could easily be adapted for corded or stuffed quilting. Some of the problems encountered in wadded quilting, particularly that of manipulating bulky layers of fabric on the machine, would not apply, as the filling is inserted after the quilting is completed.

129   Child's dungarees in brown, orange and green leather. The quilted pineapple motifs give a hard wearing protection to the knees
Maureen Magrath

118

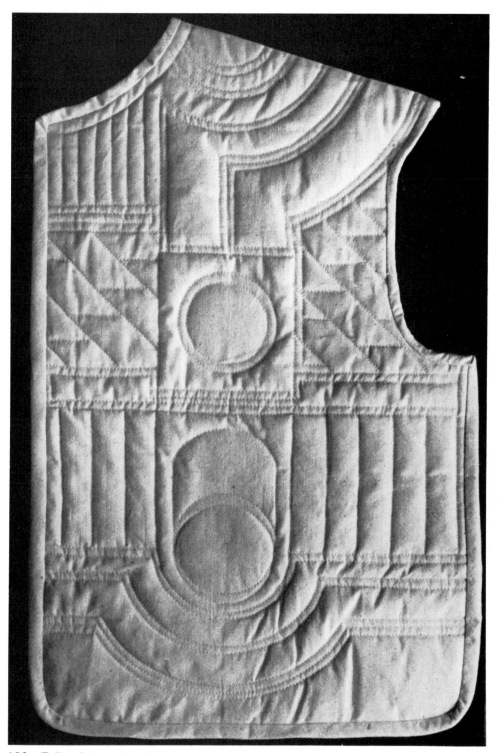

130 Toile of sleeveless jacket
Rozanne Hawksley. Instructions for
making the jacket pages 121–123

instructions for making the sleeveless jacket, kimono jacket and apron dress

These are all simple garments, without controlled shaping, ie they do not have darts or curved body seams. Turnings are not allowed for in the diagrams but the advised seam allowance is given with each draft. The quilting process draws up the fabric approximately 2.5 cm (1 in.) per garment section and this has been allowed for. The garments are drafted to a medium size, corresponding to a size 14 (92 cm/36 in.) bust.

131 and 132   Variations on the sleeveless jacket.

131   Abstract quilted design

132   Jacket with contour quilting on printed fabric and laced side fastening instead of seams

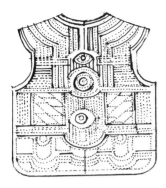

sleeveless jacket

The quilting

The jacket is quilted on the machine in wadded quilting. A tailor's chalk crayon is used for marking the design. For the quilting follow the directions given in the chapter on wadded quilting.

133 and 134 Back and front view of sleeveless jacket showing slightly assymmetric design.

Making up

1　When quilting is completed (and, if necessary, stretched to remove puckers) cut out all the pattern pieces in quilted fabric and lining. Seam allowances – 2.5 cm (1 in.) on shoulder and side seams; 15 mm ($\frac{1}{2}$ in.) on armholes, neck edge, centre front and hem.

2　Putting right sides of material together, join side and shoulder seams.

3　Repeat for lining.

4　With wrong sides together, and keeping lining loose, baste lining to top fabric along centre front, side seams and armholes.

5　Excess fullness in lining should be eased in along top and bottom of garment, or taken up in a small pleat at centre shoulder and centre hem at the front; and centre neck and centre hem at the back.

6　Bind with crossway strip 3 cm ($1\frac{1}{2}$ in.) wide, including turnings, by placing binding on garment edges, right sides facing and stitching together 15 mm ($\frac{1}{2}$ in.) in from edge, easing round curves. Trim and snip round curves, turn binding over on to wrong side of garment and slip hem to lining. Alternatively, the side seam may be left open and bound, and the sides laced or tied together decoratively.

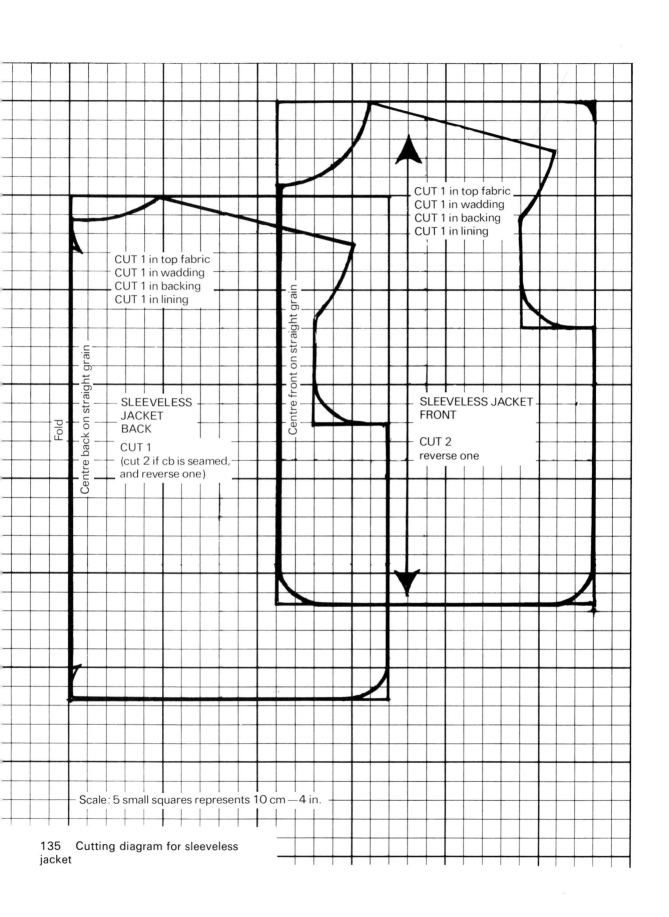

CUT 1 in top fabric
CUT 1 in wadding
CUT 1 in backing
CUT 1 in lining

CUT 1 in top fabric
CUT 1 in wadding
CUT 1 in backing
CUT 1 in lining

Centre back on straight grain

Centre front on straight grain

Fold

SLEEVELESS
JACKET
BACK

CUT 1
(cut 2 if cb is seamed,
and reverse one)

SLEEVELESS JACKET
FRONT

CUT 2
reverse one

Scale: 5 small squares represents 10 cm — 4 in.

135   Cutting diagram for sleeveless
jacket

kimono jacket

The illustrations show details of the jacket made up in mattress ticking and the design has been built up using the stripes as a basis. The design can be drawn on with a crayon, using a ruler and cardboard templates. The quilting is worked in two stages, the design units being stuffed and corded first, then the whole being mounted over a thick synthetic wadding and completed in wadded quilting. All stitching can be done on the machine if desired.

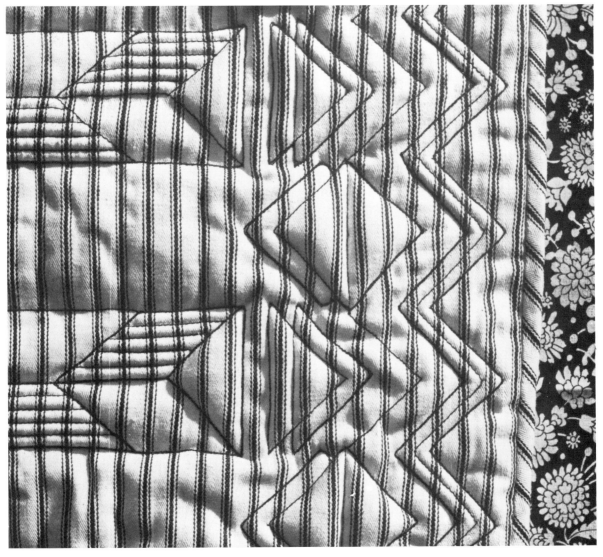

136   Detail of quilting on kimono jacket

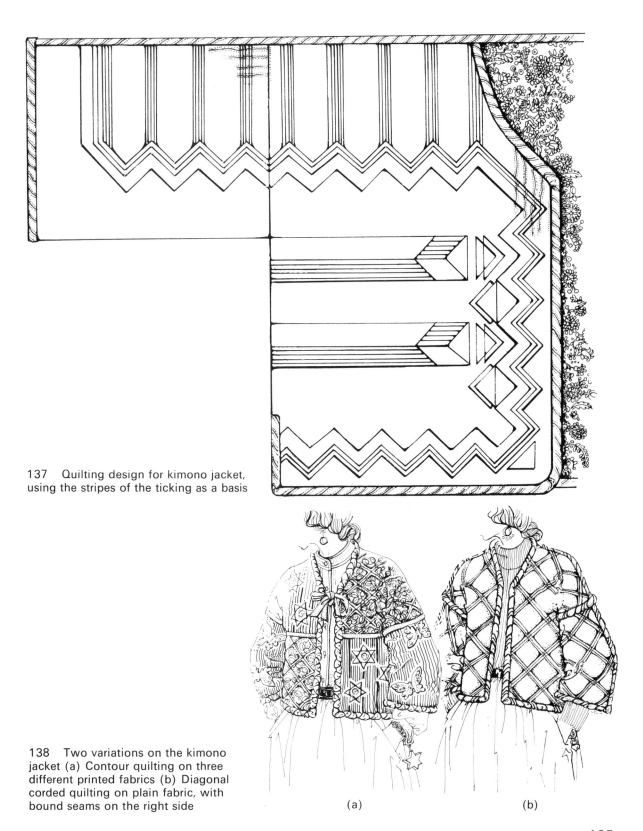

137 Quilting design for kimono jacket, using the stripes of the ticking as a basis

138 Two variations on the kimono jacket (a) Contour quilting on three different printed fabrics (b) Diagonal corded quilting on plain fabric, with bound seams on the right side

(a)

(b)

Making up the jacket

1   When quilting is complete cut out all pattern pieces with the following allowances — 2.5 cm (1 in.) on side seams, lower and armhole edge of sleeve and armhole edge of jacket; 15 mm ($\frac{1}{2}$ in.) on upper sleeve edge, sleeve hem, shoulder, neck, centre front and hem of jacket.

2   With right sides together, join sleeve fronts to jacket fronts, and sleeve backs to jacket back.

3   Repeat with lining.

4   With right sides facing join underarm seams and side seam of jacket to top of slit (A).

5   Baste in lining as for sleeveless jacket.

6   With right side of jacket outward, and crossway binding in position, starting at shoulder neck edge (B) stitch through all thicknesses of material down front, along hem, up opposite front to corresponding point at shoulder neck edge. Turn binding over and hem to lining.

7   Starting at sleeve edge (C) and with binding strip in position, stitch along upper sleeve, along shoulder, across back neck, along opposite shoulder and upper sleeve. Turn binding over and hem to lining.

8   Bind sleeve hem.

It is important that stages 6, 7 and 8 should be carried out in the right order.

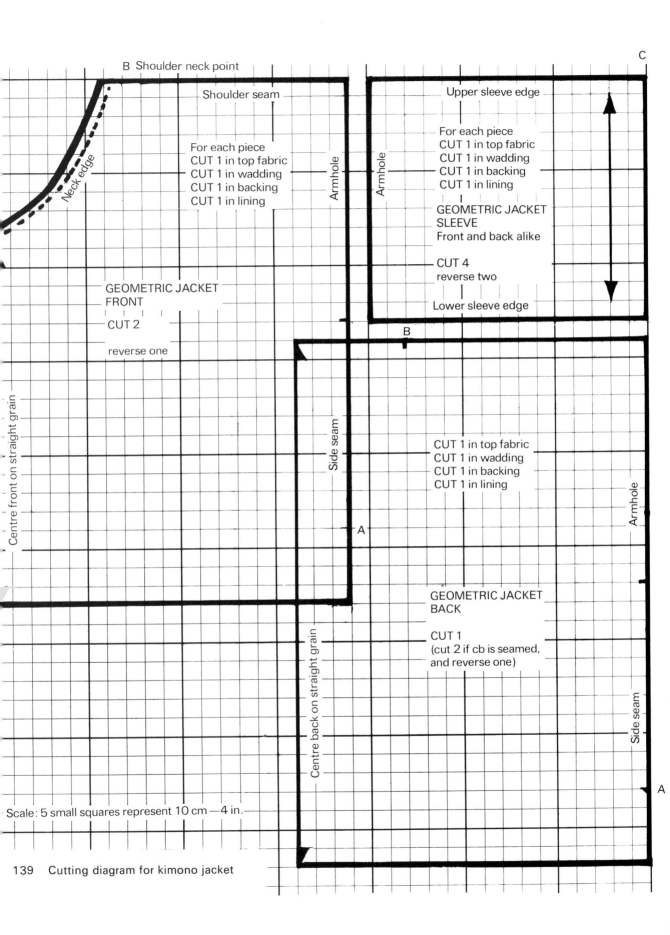

B Shoulder neck point

Shoulder seam

Neck edge

For each piece
CUT 1 in top fabric
CUT 1 in wadding
CUT 1 in backing
CUT 1 in lining

Armhole

Armhole

Upper sleeve edge

C

For each piece
CUT 1 in top fabric
CUT 1 in wadding
CUT 1 in backing
CUT 1 in lining

GEOMETRIC JACKET
SLEEVE
Front and back alike

CUT 4
reverse two

Lower sleeve edge

B

GEOMETRIC JACKET
FRONT

CUT 2

reverse one

Centre front on straight grain

Side seam

A

CUT 1 in top fabric
CUT 1 in wadding
CUT 1 in backing
CUT 1 in lining

Armhole

GEOMETRIC JACKET
BACK

CUT 1
(cut 2 if cb is seamed,
and reverse one)

Centre back on straight grain

Side seam

Scale: 5 small squares represent 10 cm — 4 in.

A

139   Cutting diagram for kimono jacket

the apron dress

The illustration shows a detail of the bodice quilted on calico. As in the kimono jacket the quilting is worked in two stages, the design being stuffed and corded for extra emphasis before wadded quilting is carried out.

140   Front bodice of the apron dress, showing the quilting completed.

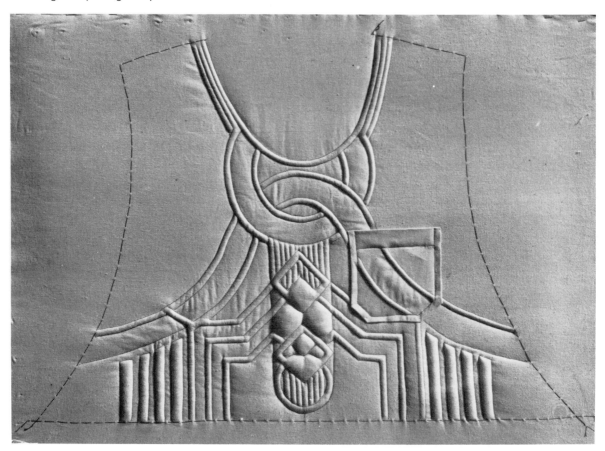

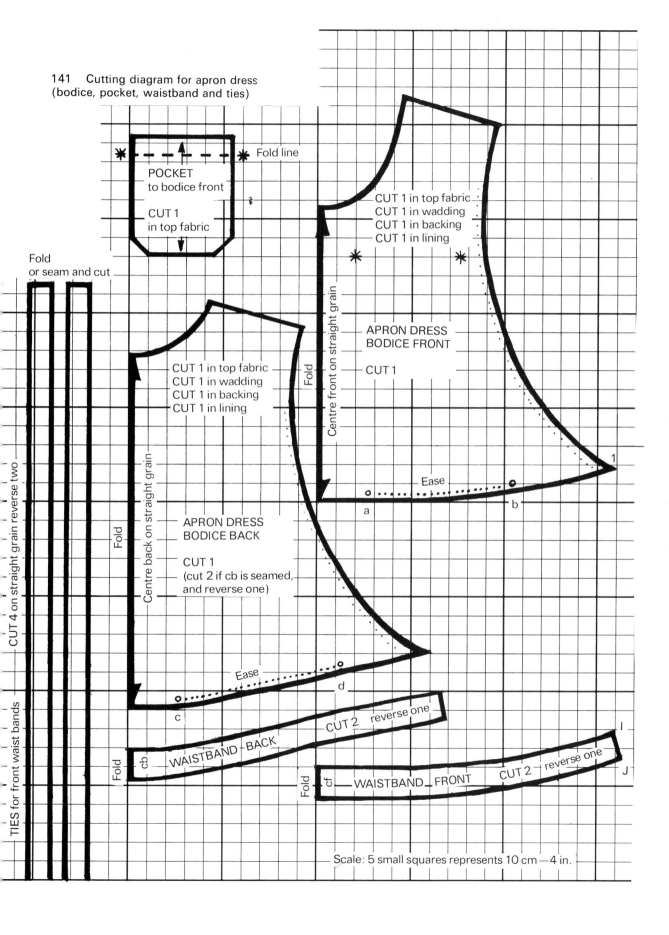

141 Cutting diagram for apron dress
(bodice, pocket, waistband and ties)

POCKET
to bodice front

CUT 1
in top fabric

Fold line

Fold
or seam and cut

CUT 1 in top fabric
CUT 1 in wadding
CUT 1 in backing
CUT 1 in lining

Centre front on straight grain

Fold

**APRON DRESS
BODICE FRONT**

CUT 1

Ease

1

a   b

CUT 1 in top fabric
CUT 1 in wadding
CUT 1 in backing
CUT 1 in lining

Centre back on straight grain

Fold

**APRON DRESS
BODICE BACK**

CUT 1
(cut 2 if cb is seamed,
and reverse one)

Ease

d

c

CUT 2   reverse one

WAISTBAND – BACK

Fold

cb

CUT 2 — reverse one

I

WAISTBAND – FRONT

Fold

cf

J

CUT 4 on straight grain reverse two

TIES for front waist bands

Scale: 5 small squares represents 10 cm — 4 in.

Making up

When bodice front is quilted cut out all pattern pieces with the following seam allowances.

1   Shoulders, bodice waist and skirt waist 2.5 cm (1 in.); all edges 15 mm ($\frac{1}{2}$ in.) and hem 5 cm (2 in.)

2   Fold over top of pocket and stitch 2 cm ($\frac{3}{4}$ in.) from edge. Fold under sides and bottom of pocket and top stitch to left side of bodice matching quilting design.

3   Baste lining to front bodice.

4   Join shoulder seams.

5   Bind neck and sides of bodice, easing fabric into binding on curved edges of side seams by running a gathered thread between points A and B and C and D.

6   Make skirt pockets and top stitch in position.

7   Starting 5 cm (2 in.) up from hem line make two or three tucks or rows of corded quilting.

8   Gather front skirt between points E and F and back skirt between points G and H so that bodice pieces fit waistbands.

9   Hem skirt and bind side edges of skirt.

10   With wrong sides together stitch bodice front to top of waist band and skirt front to bottom of same waistband, joining I to I and J to J. Trim excess fabric, stitch waistband lining into place.

11   Repeat for back.

12   Make up four ties and attach to each end of front and back waistband.

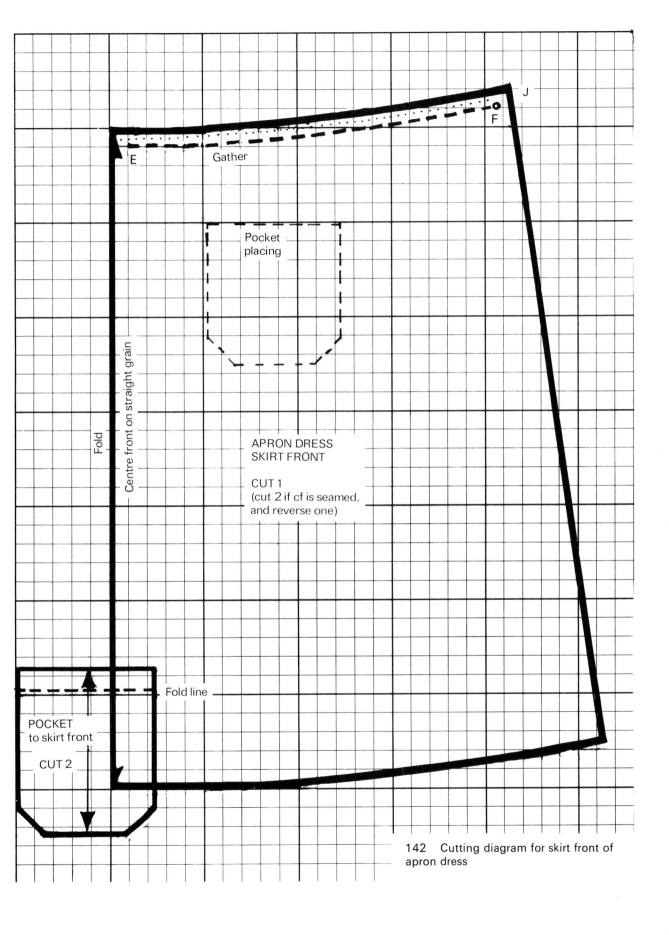

142 Cutting diagram for skirt front of apron dress

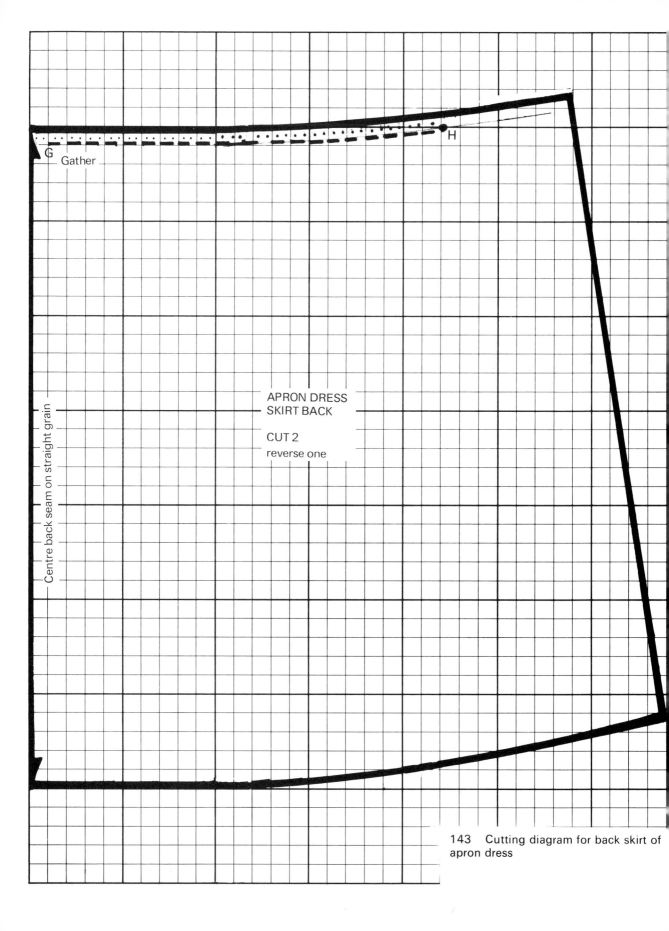

G Gather

H

Centre back seam on straight grain

APRON DRESS
SKIRT BACK

CUT 2
reverse one

143 Cutting diagram for back skirt of apron dress

144   Apron dress with quilted bodice.
Rozanne Hawksley

accessories

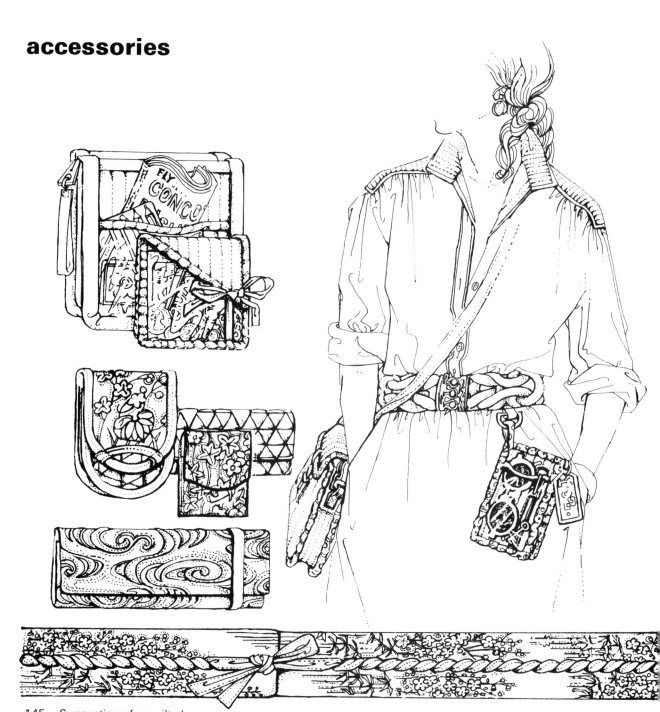

145 Suggestions for quilted
accessories Rozanne Hawksley. The
travel bag, make-up bag and spectacle
case are made up in transparent PVC
with quilted bindings

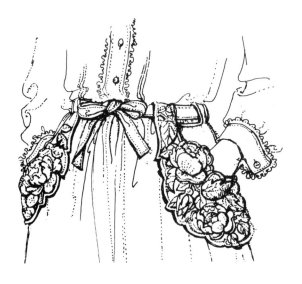

146 Detachable pockets to hang on a
belt. Design 'A Pocket full of Posies'
Rozanne Hawksley

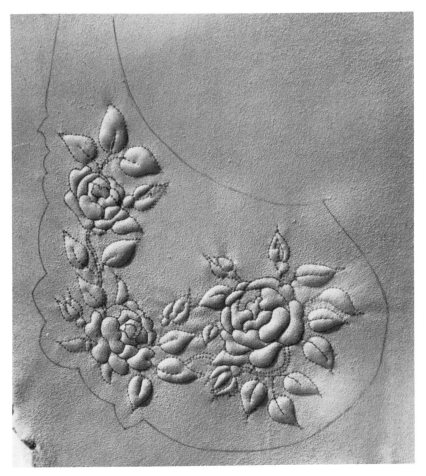

147 The design, quilted on
washable suede, completed
before cutting out the pocket

Figure 126 shows variations on a theme of detachable suede pockets to be slipped over a belt and worn with a plain skirt. The worked detail (figure 147) is on washable suede, worked with a pure silk thread in back stitch. A leather needle was used. These are available for both hand and machine stitching. The design should be put on with a waterproof laundry marking pen as chalk and crayon do not show up well enough on suede. The design was stitched by hand through the suede and a calico backing, before being stuffed.

Making up

1   When quilting is complete cut out front of pocket in suede and cotton lawn lining and back of pocket in suede, with 6 mm ($\frac{1}{4}$ in.) seam allowance.

2   Place front pocket right side up with lining in place behind it, on top of back pocket also right side up. Sew from A to B through all thicknesses. Trim away lawn lining between leather edges.

3   Bind top curve of pocket front from C to B using a strip of suede about 15 mm ($\frac{1}{2}$ in.) wide, top stitched into place. Cut strip 15 mm ($\frac{1}{2}$ in.) longer than top curve, but stop the stitching 15 mm ($\frac{1}{2}$ in.) back from point B. Bind top of pocket back from A-C-D-B. Between points A and C binding will enclose top of pocket front and pocket back. At point B take surplus binding round to back of pocket – neaten.

4   Fold pocket straps over towards the back and stitch or fasten to form loops which slip over a belt.

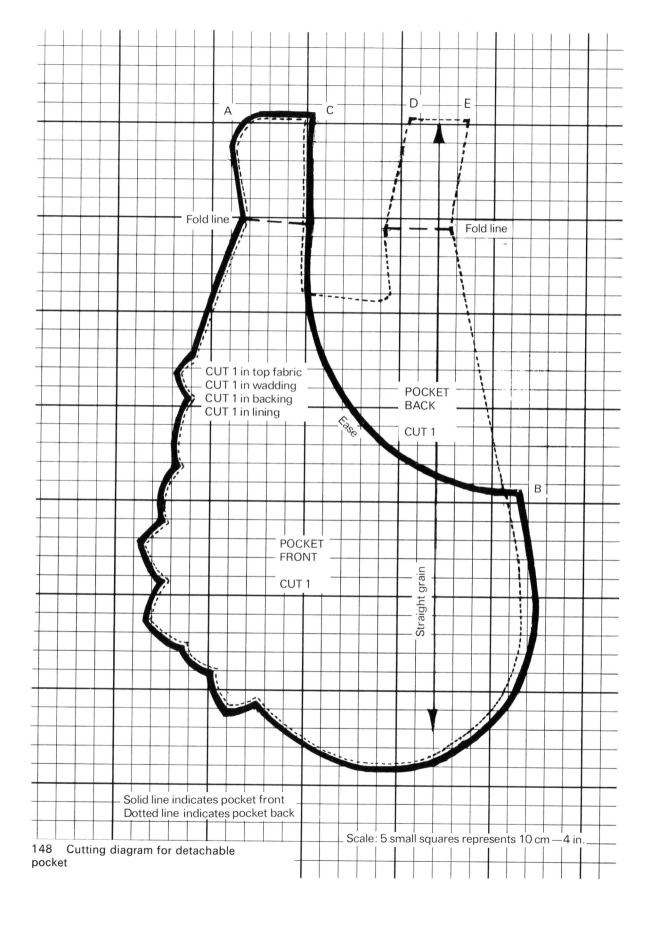

A   C   D   E

Fold line

Fold line

CUT 1 in top fabric
CUT 1 in wadding
CUT 1 in backing
CUT 1 in lining

POCKET
BACK

CUT 1

Ease

B

POCKET
FRONT

CUT 1

Straight grain

Solid line indicates pocket front
Dotted line indicates pocket back

Scale: 5 small squares represents 10 cm —4 in.

148   Cutting diagram for detachable
pocket

Making up
Silk purse (figure 149a).

When quilting is complete
1   Cut out all pattern pieces as shown in figure 149b. No turnings are allowed for and all stitching is carried out 6 mm ($\frac{1}{4}$ in.) from edge.
2   Tack along fold lines a and b.
3   The gusset should have an interlining if it is not quilted. Baste all thicknesses together and tack along centre fold line. Stitch purse front on to gusset, wrong sides together. Trim, snip round curves.
4   Attach binding by stitching it right side down on purse front, following previous line of stitching. Turn binding over and hem to gusset.
5   Bind top edge of gusset and purse front.
6   Attach purse back and flap section to gusset and bind as in 3 and 4.
7   Put on fastening of choice (press stud, toggle, button, etc). Plaited silk cord could be used to make a handle attached to the back of the purse, or made on a bigger scale the purse could become a shoulder bag, with the addition of leather or webbing strap.

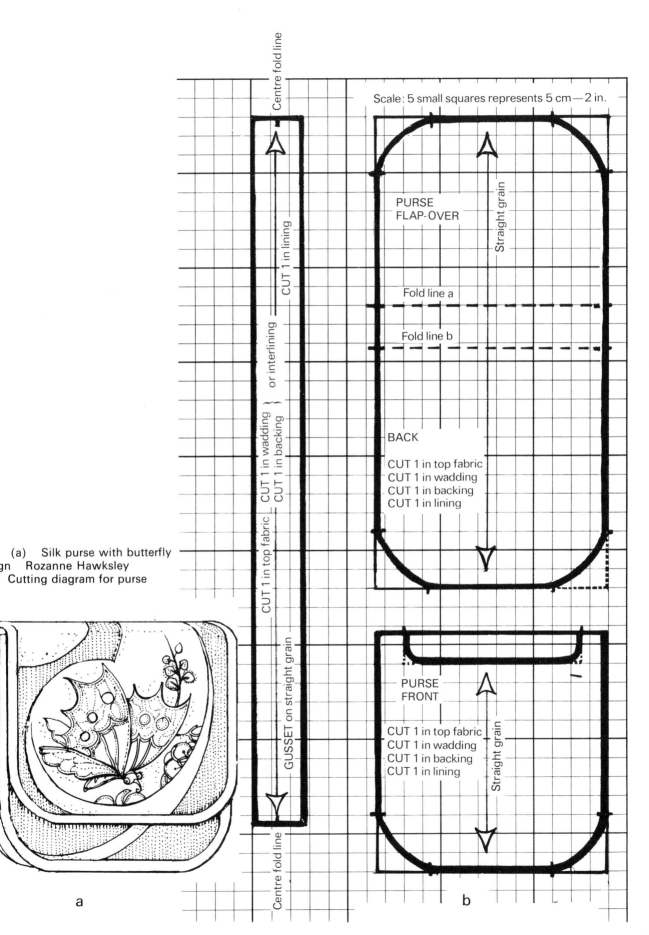

Scale: 5 small squares represents 5 cm — 2 in.

Centre fold line

CUT 1 in lining

or interlining
CUT 1 in wadding
CUT 1 in backing

CUT 1 in top fabric
CUT 1 in backing

CUT 1 in top fabric

GUSSET on straight grain

Centre fold line

PURSE
FLAP-OVER

Straight grain

Fold line a

Fold line b

BACK

CUT 1 in top fabric
CUT 1 in wadding
CUT 1 in backing
CUT 1 in lining

PURSE
FRONT

Straight grain

CUT 1 in top fabric
CUT 1 in wadding
CUT 1 in backing
CUT 1 in lining

49 (a) Silk purse with butterfly
design Rozanne Hawksley
(b) Cutting diagram for purse

a

b

150 Headdress worn by the 71st
Punjabis Regiment in the first world war,
consisting of the pugri (a length of
cotton) and the khali, a quilted cap with
metal thread embroidery

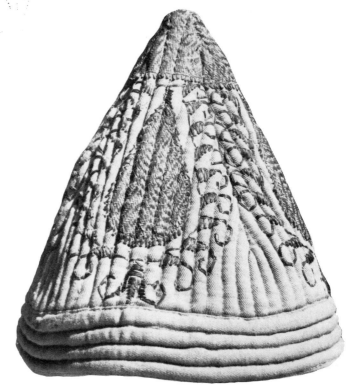

151 Detail of the khali

152 Ideas for quilted kimonos.
Rozanne Hawksley

Technical hints

equipment

(a) For quilting by hand

A rectangular frame which consists of two bars with a webbing tape attached (rails) and two flat strips of wood (stretchers). The length of the webbing controls the width of fabric which may be quilted, and the frame is generally sold by this length eg 46 cm (18 in.) tape, 61 cm (24 in.) tape. Frames can usually be bought up to 76 cm (30 in.) tape, but large frames for bed quilts, which are normally 228 cm (90 in.) can be made quite simply to the same pattern.

Although not always essential, a frame is useful in that it leaves both hands free for the actual stitching – one hand can remain underneath the work to receive the needle as it is pushed through from the top. It also holds the different layers securely in their correct positions.

A round frame for small pieces of work.

Two pairs of scissors; one large pair for cutting out and a small pair (possibly curved) for trimming threads.

Plenty of fine needles; several can be threaded up at once in order to save interrupting the rhythm of the work once it gets going, and they can also be used instead of pins on fabric which marks easily.

Thimble.

A rug needle for marking designs; a tracing wheel and tailor's chalk for the same purpose.

Templates. These may be metal ones, which can be bought in a variety of shapes and sizes, or card cut to your own design. When making your own template, it is important to measure and cut really accurately.

Stanley knife (craft knife) for cutting card.

(b) For quilting by machine

A quilting foot with gauge; also a raised seam attachment where this is available with the machine.

A round frame for free running.

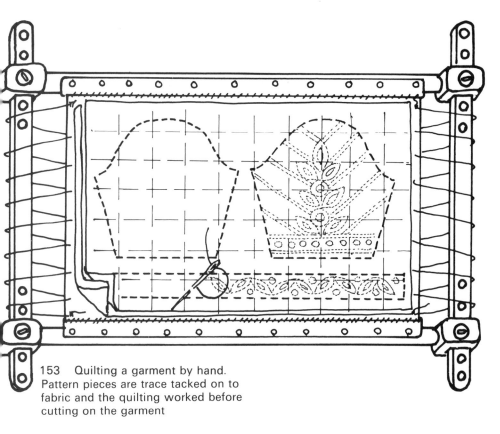

153 Quilting a garment by hand.
Pattern pieces are trace tacked on to
fabric and the quilting worked before
cutting on the garment

materials

Where possible it is recommended that fabrics made from natural fibres are used for quilting. This is particularly important where elaborate hand quilting is being contemplated, as most synthetic fabrics are too springy to give the controlled undulating surface which can be obtained with cotton, silk or fine linen. For geometric designs worked on the machine, however, they are practicable and even PVC can, with care, be quilted.

For fillings, on the other hand, the present day synthetic waddings are ideal. In the past a variety of fillings was used including wadding, cotton wool, carded sheep's wool or old blankets, but *Terylene* or *Tricel* wadding have the advantage of being lightweight, washable and quick drying. For less padded quilting, domette is also light and easy to sew through, but is only guaranteed for dry cleaning.

If a dark fabric is being quilted, using a white filling and stitching by hand, the look of the work is sometimes marred by small flecks of the filling being pulled through by the needle. This can be overcome by putting a layer of organdie or muslin immediately under the top fabric, which will stop the filling pulling through. Alternatively, black domette can be used as a filler.

ironing

Fabrics which are to be quilted should be ironed thoroughly before the layers are tacked together, as it is impossible to get deep creases out after the quilting has been done.

tacking

This should be done from the centre out on small pieces of work and in horizontal and vertical rows on larger pieces (figure 154). It is vital, especially in machine quilting not to skimp on tacking, or the various layers of fabric will move during the working, resulting in unsightly bubbles and wrinkles. The only exception is if a very delicate fabric is being used which would mark badly. In this case it should be possible to pin the layers together with very fine needles until the quilting is completed. This was done with the waistcoat in figure 50.

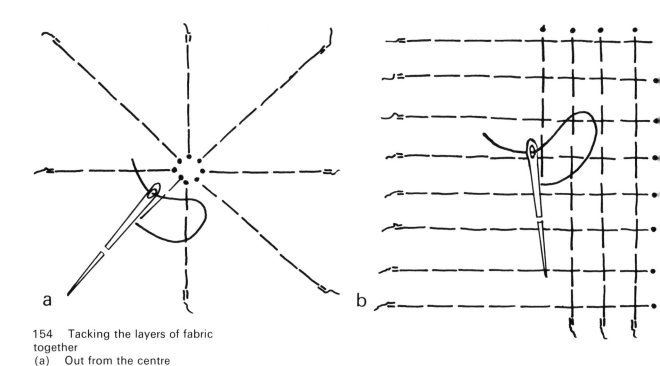

154   Tacking the layers of fabric
together
(a)   Out from the centre
(b)   In a horizontal and vertical grid

144

155, 156 Details of two novel bed quilts based on landscapes
155 Cover for a small boy's bed which can be used during the day as a setting for model cars. Made for her son by Barbara Siedlecka

156 Rural landscape. The cover is highly padded and all the details such as trees, building and animals made by hand in fabric and thread   Susie Pile

marking designs

Designs should be marked on the right side of the top fabric by one of the following methods.

(a) *Needlemarking* This is the cleanest way of putting on the design. It is sometimes called 'scratching' but this is a misnomer as the fabric is never scratched, merely indented. This method is particularly suitable when designs are being built up round templates, or with a ruler. A rug needle is used, never one with a point, as this would damage the surface of the material. It helps to push the needle into a cork, or to thread a length of wool through the eye in order to get a firm grip on the needle while marking. The needle should be held almost parallel with the fabric, with the forefinger outstretched to insert pressure near the tip of the needle, and a clean single indented line made round the template (figure 157c). When using a frame, mark only as much as can be reached comfortably, or if the work is being handled as in machine quilting, as much as can be worked in one sitting. Most fabrics which are suitable for quilting will retain an indented line long enough for the stitching to be completed. Synthetics are too springy, and if they are being used are better chalked, although a test should always be made to ensure that the chalk will brush off without leaving a mark. Tailor's chalk should be sharpened to a fine edge, or a well pointed dressmaker's marking pencil may be used, and the drawing done round templates as above. Traditionally, on dark fabrics sharpened dry soap was used.

(b) *Pinging* Long straight lines can be 'pinged'. Rub a length of string with chalk, and with the help of another person hold it taut immediately above the position of the required line. Pick up the string in the middle and let it go with a sharp 'ping' so that a perfectly accurate straight line is transferred to the fabric.

(c) *Perforating* The design can be transferred from paper on to the fabric by running over the lines of the design with a tracing wheel (originally a spur was used) (figure 157b). With many fabrics this dotted line will last long enough for the work or a portion of it to be completed, as with needlemarking, but if a more permanent pattern is required a very hard sharp pencil can be used to mark through the holes in the tracing paper, or the design may be pounced and painted. Should the lines of the design be too intricate for the use of a tracing wheel a darning needle can be used for the pricking. Perforation can also be done on the machine, with the foot on or as for free running but without a thread. In fact, with a simple machined pattern the actual quilting can be carried out through paper which is then torn away, but this should not be tried with an intricate design.

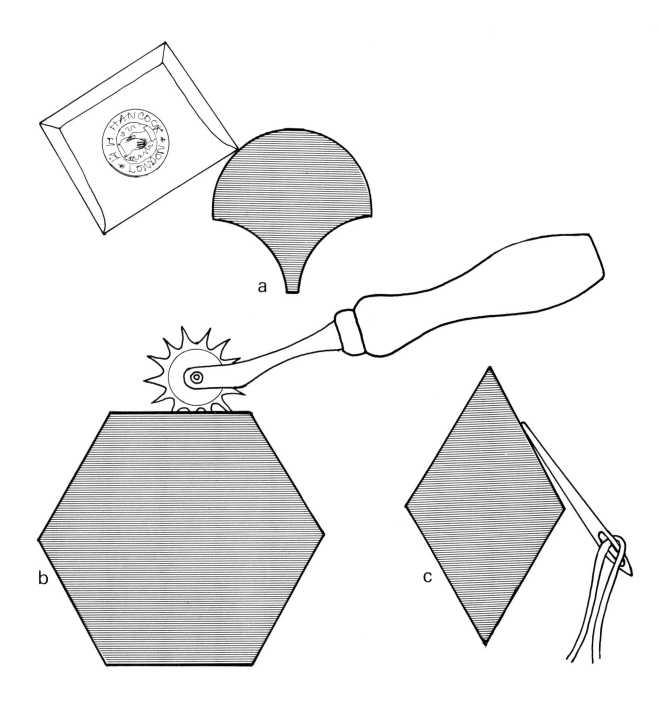

157 Marking round a template
(a) With sharp tailor's chalk
(b) With a tracing wheel
(c) With a rug needle

(d)   Designs can be drawn freehand on the top layer in paint or crayon.

(e)   *Embroidery carbon paper* (sometimes sold as tracing paper) With care, this method can be quite successful. Place the carbon working side down, between the drawing and the fabric, and press through the lines of the design with a fine, hard point. (A ball point pen which has run out of ink is ideal.) Or, run over the design with a tracing wheel. Embroidery carbon is available in a number of colours, for light or dark fabric.

(f)   *Transfers*   Commercial transfers may be ironed on to the fabric. Banal designs can be made more interesting by cutting up the transfers and moving the pieces around to build up one's own design.

(g)   Some traditional quilting, especially in America, was marked by printing with a wood or metal block. As a makeshift, experiments could be made with fabric inks or dyes (available from art shops) on say, pastry cutters, building up patterns as with templates and printing them on to the fabric.

The first three methods should be carried out after the different layers have been tacked together as they are only semi-permanent. The other methods can be done before tacking.

Methods (d), (e) and (f) are not really suitable if the quilting is being done in running stitch as the line will show in the spaces between the stitches. With back stitch, chain stitch or machining the problem does not arise, providing the marked line is kept fine enough.

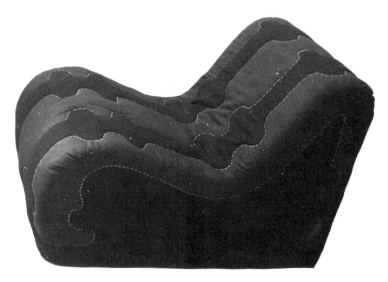

158   Chair cover quilted on the machine by Doreen Nartey. 'Automatic' embroidery stitches have been used

159 *Fern Quilt* (254 cm × 254 cm: 100 in. × 100 in.) Bets Ramsey. The design is based on a one-line poem by her husband, Paul Ramsey, which reads 'Fern, a tracing of air.' The quilt is in white and pale blue cotton with green appliqué. Owned by Dr and Mrs Earl Campbell Jr of Chattanooga

stitching by hand

for wadded quilting

To start – bring the needle up on a line of the design 'losing' the knotted end of the thread in the filling. For a really secure start make a small back stitch and go back into it splitting the thread. All stitches are worked from the right side of the work.

(a)   Running   It is essential that the stitch should pierce all three layers, so for the inexperienced quilter a stab stitch (figure 160a) is recommended. With more experience it is possible to make a run of several stitches before pulling the needle through as in ordinary running. This is done by holding the left hand underneath the work to feel the needle coming through and to guide it back to the surface, while the right hand on top of the work pushes the needle along. This is the method used by professional quilters, but needs a lot of practice to perfect.

(b)   Back stitch   This too is best worked in a stabbing fashion (figure 160b).

(c)   Chain   When the quilting is held in the hand chain stitch can be worked in one movement (figure 159c), but when the work is in a frame two separate stabbing movements must be made.

(d)   'Pearl'   There are two ways of achieving a pearl effect. One is simply to work a very short back stitch in a thick twisted cotton (figure 160d); the other is worked as follows: take a small single stitch, but before drawing it up pass the needle underneath from right to left and then tighten up the stitch. Again, use a thick thread and a short stitch for the best effect (figure 160e).

Finishing off threads: run needle through padding and bring up further along on the marked line. Take needle down over one thread of the material and run through padding again. Repeat until end of thread is used up. The minute stitches on the surface will be completely hidden as the work proceeds.

Stitching by hand for other types of quilting

When stitching flat, corded or stuffed quilting it is not necessary to stab stitch as there is no thick filling to be gone through.

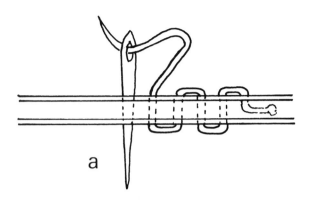

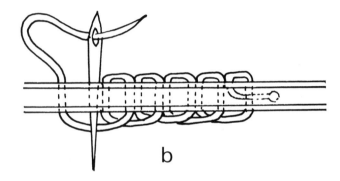

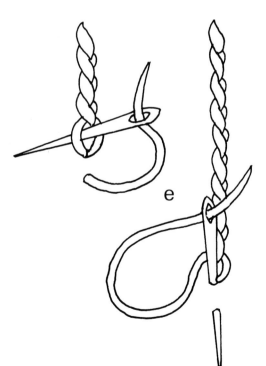

160 Stitches used in hand quilting
(a) Running
(b) Back stitch
(c) Chain stitch
(d) Pearl effect achieved by working
small stitches in thick thread
(e) Two stages in a true pearl stitch

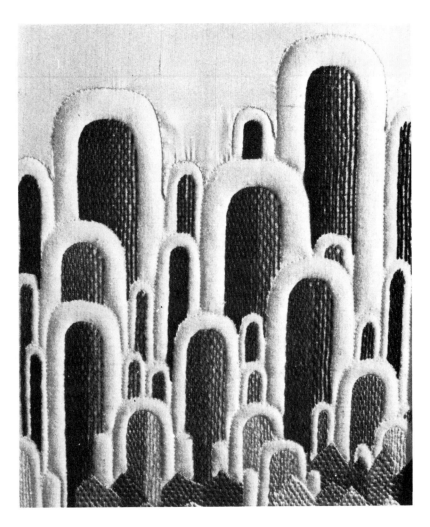

161   Panel combining quilting and
surface stitchery   Marion Gilling

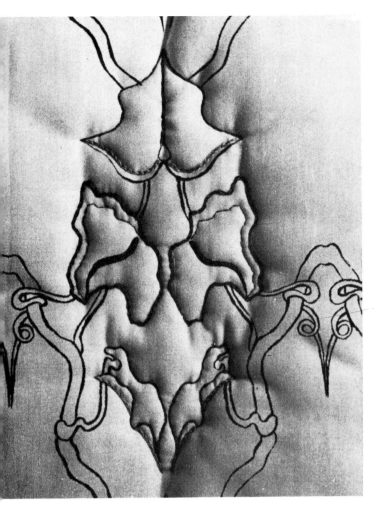

163 Panel with various techniques, including quilting   Anita-Marie Digby

162 Detail of a design. Quilting in back stitch and chain stitch combined with screen printing   Marion Hicks

quilting on the machine

Use the quilting foot supplied with the machine. For straight lines and simple repeats insert adjustable gauge into the quilting foot using it to maintain equal distances between lines of stitching (figure 33). This keeps the marking of lines down to a minimum, and adds to the freshness of the work. For non-parallel and more intricate lines remove the gauge to make the work more manoeuverable and the pattern easier to see.

Size of needle depends on the type of fabric used and thickness of work. Heavy padding requires a strong needle. When machining leather or suede insert a special leather needle.

Length of stitch will also depend largely on the scale of the work, but generally speaking a medium length stitch with a slightly loose tension is satisfactory. PVC requires a long stitch, or the perforated fabric tears away like a stamp. PVC sometimes sticks under the foot, and the stitches build up. This can be overcome by putting talcum powder, french chalk or a smear of oil on the top surface before stitching.

With wadded quilting, loosen pressure on presser foot and always make sure that the layers are well tacked together. To ensure further that the materials do not ride, hold the work out with the hands on either side of the foot as the stitching proceeds. Stitch alternate lines in opposite directions (figure 164).

As well as straight stitching quilting may be carried out in satin stitch or with set 'automatic' stitches. These could be combined with free stitching to build up geometric filling within shapes, or to give variety of line.

Cable stitch gives a bolder line than ordinary machining and is worked in the following way:

Fill the spool with an unstranded embroidery cotton such as pearl. Loosen the tension screw on the spool case to enable the thread to feed out smoothly. Thread the top of the machine with normal sewing cotton or silk with a slightly tighter tension than usual. Work upside down so that the pearl cotton is on the right side. The stitch has the appearance of a neat couched line. Experiments can be made with length of stitch as this alters the appearance of the stitch considerably.

Free running stitch

This is done with the foot removed and the feed dog lowered, the work being held taut in a round frame when possible. If the quilting is very bulky a frame may be impracticable, but the work can be mounted on vanishing muslin or even held out flat with both hands. This type of work needs practice, but does enable far more intricate work to be carried out on the machine.

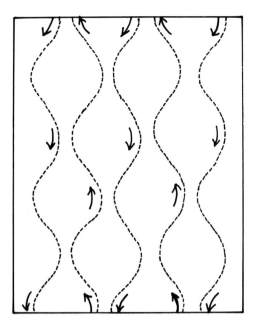

164 Quilting on the machine. Work
alternate rows in opposite directions

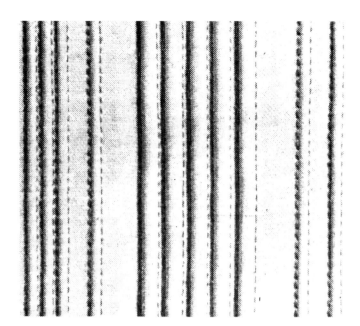

165 Cording made with the twin
needle and raised seam attachment

Areas of free running may be combined with stitching carried
out with the foot on.

Stitching with twin needles gives an effect of cording, and, used
in conjunction with the raised seam attachment, gives a true
cording (figure 165). Alternatively, tucks can be stitched in the
normal way and then threaded with cord.

Large articles in wadded quilting are difficult to manipulate on
the machine. It is sometimes possible to roll the spare fabric on the
right of the needle tightly, to make the work more manœuverable,
or the quilting could be carried out in blocks and later assembled
(see lap quilting, figure 49). Stuffed quilting is ideal for big projects
on the machine as all the stitching can be completed before any
bulky stuffing is inserted.

Clean the machine frequently when quilting as fluff builds up
quickly round the spool case. Oil regularly for smooth running.

166 Commercial quilting in chain
stitch on the Cornely machine

167 Sampler by Julia Roberts
combines quilted lettering with
patchwork

168 *California* quilt, (237 cm × 257 cm: 93 in. × 101 in.)   Joan Schulze. This is hand-quilted and made in cotton, silk and muslin. The landscape area is one piece of cotton material 'batiked' with procion dyes

169 Quilted hanging, In the Shadow of His Wing (193 cm × 99 cm: 76 in. × 39 in.) Doris Hoover. The hanging combines print, patchwork and appliqué and is hand quilted. By courtesy of the North Carolina Museum of Art

Suppliers

Great Britain

Materials and sewing accessories

McCullock & Wallis Ltd, 25/26 Dering Street, London W1R 0BH
for butter muslin, mull, organdie, calico, domette, wadding, iron-on
interlining and reasonably priced cotton fabrics, printed and plain.
Also piping cord, binding and threads for machine and hand work;
needles, pins, scissors, tailor's chalk, marking pencils and tracing
wheels

John Lewis & Company Ltd, Oxford Street, London W1A 1EX
for a wide selection of fabrics; also beads, interlinings and sewing
accessories as above

Liberty & Company Limited, Regent Street, London W1R 6BA
for a wide selection of fabrics; also suede and leather

Mace and Nairn, 89 Crane Street, Salisbury, Wiltshire
for a wide selection of fabrics and sewing accessories

Christine Riley, 53 Barclay Street, Stonehaven, Kincardineshire
AB3 2AR
for a wide selection of fabrics and sewing accessories; also beads

Limericks, Hamlet Court Road, Westcliff-on-Sea, Essex
for reasonably priced cotton sheeting up to 90 in. wide in white
and a good selection of colours

The Felt and Hessian Shop, 34 Greville Street, London EC1
for felt in a wide range of strong colours suitable for shadow quilting

Honeywill Ltd, Leather Merchants, 22a Fouberts Place, London W1
for suede and leather

B & G Leathercloth Limited, 71 Fairfax Road, London NW6 4EE
for all types of PVC

Beads

Fred Aldous Limited, The Handicrafts Centre, 37 Lever Street, Manchester M60 1UX

Ells & Farrier Limited, 5 Princes Street, London W1R 8PH

Sesame Ventures, Greenham Hall, Wellington, Somerset

USA

For a wide variety of materials, threads and accessories

American Thread Corporation, 90 Park Avenue, New York

Bucky King Embroideries Unlimited, 121 South Drive, Pittsburgh, Pennsylvania 15238

Yarn Bazaar, Yarncrafts Limited, 3146 M Street North West Washington, DC

Beads

Amar Pearl and Bead Co. Inc, 19001 Stringway, Long Island City, NY

Hollander Bead and Novelty Corporation, 25 West 37 Street, New York 18, NY

Leather

Aerolyn Fabrics Inc, 380 Broadway, New York

Index

Figures in *italics* refer to illustration numbers